Worzel Wooface

My quite very actual book

Catherine Pickles

ISBN-13: 978-1508549857
ISBN: 1508549850

DEDICATION

For Mike, Sam and Sarah.

To everyone who has ever rescued
a dog, rather than buying;
to all the people who originally followed Worzel's blog and
gave me the courage to write this book;
to my friends and neighbours, who have unwittingly found
themselves in print;

THANK YOU.

CONTENTS

FOREWORD

Worzel was one of the first dogs rescued by a new re-homing charity; Hounds First Sighthound Rescue. He'd been beaten and abused by the person who bred him, tried for working, deemed unsuitable, picked on by another dog and finally relinquished to Hounds First. He was 10 weeks old.

Worzel was adopted by the founder of Hounds First, Rachel. He was her dream dog, loved beyond words and beautifully cared for. But Worzel had previously suffered tremendous abuse that meant he was incredibly anxious, with some inexplicable and unpredictable triggers. After a significant near miss involving one of her children, Rachel found herself in a really horrendous position. She knew she had to find a different home for Worzel but founders of dog rescues don't generally re-home their own dogs; it's really not the done thing! There would be 'talk' in the rescue world and the relatively new (but immediately successful) rescue was under the microscope. There is as much envy, jealousy and back-biting in the field of dog rescue as there is in almost every walk of life and plenty of people at that time would have been quite happy to see Hounds First fail.

Rachel might have attempted to protect her own reputation or brush everything under the carpet but she put Worzel first and although this risked her standing in the rescue world, it ultimately showed that she (and Hounds First) would always put the welfare of the dogs in their care before their reputation, status or personal feelings. It's no wonder then, that Hounds First is now a thriving, much respected rescue.

An enigmatic Facebook status, a phone call to another trustee of the rescue and 3 words changed my life. 'He comes here,' I said. Worzel arrived in Suffolk both confused and highly stressed having travelled 300 miles in a series of cars that took him quickly away from Somerset and everything he knew and loved.

I promised Rachel that I would look after Worzel and more significantly in the case of this book that I would keep her and her children updated about his progress. I started a Facebook page where I put photos and short updates for them about what he'd been doing and then everything snow-balled. Worzel found his 'voice' and I found myself writing the book everyone, they say, has 'in' them. In my daydreams, the book I had 'in' me was a worthy novel full of beautiful imagery, not the somewhat bizarre mutterings of an enormous Lurcher with a mind of his own and a voice which I increasingly find I have to stop myself using. My friends and neighbours find it very actual quite confuddling!

Worzel definitely wasn't in our plans. We'd been dog fostering for a few years after the death of our much loved collie and we were waiting for the right permanent dog to come along; something small, definitely with short legs, that we could take sailing on our boat. The right dog was never going to be an enormous, anxious Lurcher with hidden depths and a centre of gravity similar to the Eiffel Tower.

So here it is; the book I never meant to write about the dog I never meant to have. The rest of this book is Worzel's - his voice, his feelings and his opinions. They aren't necessarily always my own!

JANUARY

19 January 2014

I do hope you are ok and not missing me too much. Is it a bad fing to say that I are doing betterer? I has been here a week and it's a lot quieter here and there are less people. I has my very own space and the comfy bed you did send with me. There are no loud noises most of the time so I do not be getting frightened or having hunexpected hexperiences which do freak me very out. Fings is very predictababble so I don't seem to be so jumpy and wobbly.

Everyboddedy is quite very pleased with me and there is a lot of talk about me being booful. And luffly. And a gorgeous boykin.

I are the only dog here which is a bit of an actual shame but the hoomans do give me very lots of attention and I seem to be himportant to them. I do miss some doggy compnee to be actual honest. I hope I will be getting to meet some very actual soon.

20 January 2014

There's a dad here wot never moves. He is always there. Ok. Very sometimes he do go upstairs and make splashy noises and he do go into the kitchen and come back with a cup. But otherwise, he do just sit and tap this fing in front of him. I has tried to see wot he is tapping but it does not be making much sense. When I do go near him, he doesn't do flappering or nuffink. He is the stillest hooman I has ever met. He don't be saying much either. Just sitting and tapping. Tappering and sittering. The only way you can get him to do moving is to nudge him. Then he do turn his head and maybe stroke me a little bit but I do has to be quite insistering to get his attention.

He stays up ever so late, way past my bedtime, doing this tapping. When he do get up, I has taken to following him about just to see if he does anyfink more hinteresting than tap. It seems not. He sometimes says a gentle word or two when he's up and about but nuffink sudden or loud.

When he is not tapping, he does go and do somefing called work which seems to involve him getting muddy or sandy or covered in woody fluff. It sounds like exerlent fun. When he comes home he do sit down in his chair and press the tappy fing. I think the tappy fing is called Uff. Every day he does the same fing; he sits down, presses the tappy fing and says 'Uff, I'm-knackered.' And then Uff lights up. I are not sure wot Uff is exactly or wot would happen if the man didn't tap it. Do he have to tap it to keep it going? No wonder he is very knackered all the time if he does have to work all day and then tap Uff all night to keep it alive.

Sometimes, the mum gets quite cross with the dad about Uff. Especially when she does want him to do somefing else. Then he says 'I can't. People will die.' That do make the mum steaming mad. She do say 'It's only a computer game people will not flipping die.' Then he do say 'Gimme-a-sec,' and the mum storms off in a huff because she do know that Gimme-a-sec is about 3 hours.

The mum is the person who is in charge of food so I do fink she is very quite actual himportant. She has decided that I will be having somefing called a raw diet. This mainly seems to involve having proper food like chicken wings and minced up proper meat and cheese and real stuff like that so I are actual quite very chuffed to bits about this. I do know that some dogs is fed out of a bag but the mum here does not be wanting me eating brown-balls-full-of-wheat-and-rubbish. The dad wasn't too sure about this and muttered about lots of dogs having brown-balls-full-of-wheat-and-rubbish and about it being complete and made by scientists.

The mum coulda given him some long sentences about it all but then dad woulda said 'People will die. Gimme-a-sec' so the mum made the dad go and look at my poo. To be very actual honest, I do fink the dad would have agreed to anyfink, rather than do this but the mum did do insistering. The dad fort he would have to look at a volcano of brown sticky smelly yuck but all he did see was 3 little nuggets wot did not be smelling at all and that was the very end of any harguments ever again about brown-balls-full-of-wheat-and-rubbish.

The mum do not go out of the house when everyboddedy else does. She do not be going to work or to school but very God. Help. Hanyone. who says she does nuffink or does not do work. The dad did try this recently and then he did find out how much work the mum doesn't do. So, the mum is in charge of walking, wot I do fink is the most himportant job in the house. We has started off with getting to know each other and the places around here. There are lots of fields and lanes but only one big road wot we don't go and look at very often. We wented there to test it out and did find out that I do not really mind big lorries or vans but it is a boring, smelly walk and sometimes there is rubbish and broken stuff around.

There are some very exerlent fields nearby and just recently we has been trying out wot would happen if I was letted off my lead. I are alright at coming back but the mum is struggling to find somefing that will make me do it quickerer. I has tried to actual tell her she is very quite wasting her time; there is no food and no toy wot will make me come back all quick. She is a trier though. She has taken balls, cheese, bits of meat, all sorts. The only fing we have reached a hagreement on is ball frower stick fings. As far as I are actual concerned, they is horrid. Sticks of any kind are not my friend. She took the ball frower with us a couple of days ago and to be quite actual honest, she is flippin' lucky I did come back a-very-tall. At first, the mum was hopeful that I was hexcited but then she did see I was not hexcited but very terrified and doing an actual bog off runner. The mum dropped the stick and ranned away from it. She did go and sit down in the middle of the actual field whilst I did watching her from the hedge. She did get a quite very muddy cold bum sitting there and I was actual quite happy about this. I do not know wot has happened to the hateful ball frower stick fing but it did not come back home with us. It might actual still be in the field, or maybe some dog wot is not terrified of them is playing with it.

Talking of dogs, I STILL hasn't been introduced to any. Not blinking one. I do fink this is not ok. I know there is other dogs around here because I has heard them barking and woofing. The mum do say I will meet them soon but not until I is settled and she has actual got to know me very quite well. She do say that she is going to make sure I only has positive hexperiences and it is actual early days.

21 January 2014

This house is only ever noisy for an hour in the morning and then it is bonkers crazy. This is mainly because of the fuge ginger boyman. He cannot ever, hever be finding anyfink. I do fink he can't find anyfink because he do look for fings with the very actual wrong part of his boddedy. He has gotted it into his head that his mouth can see fings. He opens his mouth and yells, 'where's my wallet and 'where's my phone.' I keep wanting to tell him that his eyeballs are not in his mouth, they is hiding under his hair. He has long, long ginger orange hair. And no eyebrows.

Maybe that's why his eyes keeping getting lost and falling into his mouth because he don't be having eyebrows to keep his eyeballs in the right place.

I FINK there is only one other smaller hooman who lives here but I is not completely sure. She do never look like the same person for very long. Currently she do have black hair and she seems to keep most of it in a muddle on her dressing table. It looks like a collection of black dogs' tails which is very actual flipping scary. I do not know where she did get all these tails from and I are very quite relieved that my tail is ginger and not black cos she might want to stick it in her hair with the others. She do not seem to like ginger as a colour at all. The fuge ginger boyman says she is really a ginger as well but she is in The Nile, so she do make her hair black and stick tails in her hair to make it look longer.

The mum here spends a lot of time tutting about the previously ginger one's hair. She do fink the black and the tails do not look nice. 'Your hair was so booful,' she do wail a lot. 'It'll all fall out if you keep dying it and straightening it and sticking those tensions in it.' But the previously ginger one says she is over 16 and it's her life and her head. I do strongly agree with the previously ginger one to be very actual honest. She can be doing wot she likes with her head, especially if she can remember she do not like ginger and that my tail is staying attached to my bum and not being putted in her hair.

23 January 2014

I still has not been to meet any doggy friends and I are seriously NOT pleased about this. I is getting a bit desperate now so I has had to try to make friends with the cats that do live here. Seems that this is the only 4 legged compnee I are allowed and It. Is. Not. Fair. I do not be know how to explain to the hoomans here that cats is ok but a cat is not a dog. I cannot be doing running and bitey-facey with a cat. Specially not this lot. There is shed loads of them and none of them is very quite right in the head. Well, Gipsy is, if you think cats should be super scary, bonk you on the nose without even waiting to see if you are going to actual do anyfink. That's about as normal as the cats do get here.

Frank might have been normal but he was a stray. It does fings to you when you don't get brought up proper. He is very clumsy and not wot you would call graceful. Sometimes people do describe graceful hooman as cat-like. Frank isn't cat-like; he is more cow-like to be actual honest. Frank is fuge. I mean IGNORMOUS. He has a really, wheely long tail with a big white tip and he swishes it about like he is auditioning for the 3 Musketeers. Frank's tail could play all the 3 Musketeers and their swords and their stunt doubles at the very quite same time. He can swipe a whole full milk carton onto the floor with the end of his own very tail. Frank can also swipe his very own actual self onto the floor as well. I did see him do it. He was rolling around on the table showing off to someboddedy and he did swish his tail and the rest of him followed right off the edge of the table. You woulda fort this was actual hembarrassing and it mighted have been but then Gipsy did not let him have an actual chance to fink this through because she did run over and bop him on the head for falling off the table. I mean, honestly... a boy should at least be able to be very actual ashamed before he does get beated up for being stoopid. I do fink Gipsy is a bit very actual harsh.

Gipsy's granddaughters also live here. There are 2 of them - Mouse and Mabel. They did both come here when they were only 5 weeks old because their mummy was very poorly-sick. Everyboddedy did hope that Gipsy, being actual related to them, might be kind and show them some ropes but she did take one look at them and frow herself through a window, taking half the curtain with her. So, the hoomans did have to bring them up. That was never going to end actual well because small kittens and puppies need their doggy mums and dads really much more than hoomans fink.

People do say that Mabel was very quite normal for a long time. She was being the most normal cat in the house. Then, the cat that was really mad did die and almost overnight, Mabel did become the House Mad Cat. She do see fings that aren't there and do panic over fings that are there but don't need panickering about. Like me. She do not like me a-very-tall. Currently, I has not never been in the same room as her. You would almost fink peoples were playing a very trick on me by saying she do be real because I has never actual set eyes on her. I promise I do not touch her but she be like those lizards that do leave their legs or tails or somefing behind as a very distraction. I walk into a room and all that is left of Mabel is clumps of fur waftering down towards the floor and making me sneeze.

Mouse has only just come back to live here. Until a month ago she had been missing for 5 years. No-one knows where she has been or wot she has been doing but she is very skinny and ill and has to be hindoors all the time. I think living here must make everyone a bit bonkers because Mouse seems to be the most normal cat here. She do not fall off furniture and she do not randomly bonk you on the nose or run away dropping bits of herself everywhere.

The good news is that I has been fishally declared cat safe. Of course I are cat safe. You wouldn't want to be anyfink else with this lot. No-one seems to care if the cats are dog safe though which is very not the right way round if you ask me. Mabel and Gipsy are very not dog safe. Gipsy you do have to keep away from. She does do over-reacting big time badly. The mum says she do like to start fights with neighbourhood cats but is actual rubbish at it and always loses which is quite very expensive. Mabel has taken to living in the shed. The mum says I should not take this personally; Mabel was odd before I did come here and as I is doing nuffink wrong, I is not to worry about it. Mum do worry about it though. She do call Mabel all kinds of names when she is trying to get her to come in for some food.

Frank and Mouse are very ok I do fink. I do let them come and say hello and touch noses with me which is really, wheely brave of me. They do not have wet noses and the first time Frank did touch my nose, he was so surprised by my wet nose he did sneeze. I forted he was going to bop me so I did run away. Everyone did laugh at me which was a bit very hembarrassing but then they did say good Wooface and make soppy noises about me being soft and luffly again.

25 January 2014

I've founded it. It has only taken me nearly a flipping week but I has founded The Bed. I knew there must be one in this here house somewhere but they has been keeping it hidded from me. I is not sure why because I can do most exerlent stuff on beds. I can do lying and rolling and jumpering about but for some reason this was not known to these peoples. Perhaps they did fink I would not like it or somefing. Maybe they fort I would be scared of it. I are not. I are not scared of beds in any way. Today I has showed them some of my best bed tricks so they do not be forgetting how exerlent I can be on a bed.

I STILL hasn't founded the other dogs round here though. I do fink if I do not meet them soon I is going to have a serious Complaint to The Management. That do be the mum. The dad is not The Management very often, although he did try to do some management about the bed fing. At first he did say, 'No Worzel on the bed.' But then I did sneak up when he was having his cuppatea and be all especially luffly boykin soppy Worzel. So we has reached a compromise. The mum says this is wot you call it when the dad do give in and everyone else do get their own way. Happarently I can be going on the bed very sometimes but wellies can't. Specially not muddy ones.

The dad isn't very good at management and the mum isn't very good at compromise. The dad says that's why we've got 4 cats.

<u>27 January 2014</u>

One of the rules currently is that I is not allowed in the kitchen but there is an actual hole near the bottom of the door and I peek through it. The hole is to allow the cats to go in and out and have an escape route. Happarently sticking your head through the hole is wot 'all the dogs do'. I don't know who all these 'all the dogs' are because there aren't any other dogs here, just me. I do know this because I are getting very actual quite lonely for other dogs and have been trying to persuade the mum to let me meet them, especially the ones who live very close that I can hear. I has been doing persuading by acting all hexcited and hinterested when I do hear them, so I do hope she do get the message actual soon. Currently, it is not working and I is getting FED. UP.

This house do smell of other dogs as well. Lots of them, so I do wonder where they are and why they are not here anymore. I do be hoping the previously ginger one with the dogs tails' in her hair do not be having anyfink to do with it. I are not allowed in her actual room because I do keep very sniffing these fings and getting them caughted on my nose and she do fink I are trying to pinch them. She can say OUT quite very loud and firmly when she do need to, even though she is actual small for a nearly growed up hooman.

The dad says that the other dogs wot I can smell in the house are somefing called foster dogs. These are homeless doggies wot have comed here to get organised or betterer or to settle them down so that they can then go to another home where they will be loved and looked after forever. They has all been Sighthounds like me and some of them have not been very actual cat friendly at all. That is why there is a hole in the bottom of the door so the cats can get away from the dog if they need to and do not be getting cornered.

The most recent foster dog was a puppy called Baldrick. Everyboddedy here do remember him fondly because he was funny and naughty. He liked to help with housework, especially if it did involve socks. Before that, there was Holly and Ivy. They was the most wonky dogs the mum has ever met. One did have fits and one did have wonky kidneys but they was luffly and very, very sweet... to hoomans. Holly was the most softest baby of a doggy hever but when she did see a cat, the mum says she did turn into Hannah the Bull Lecter. Happarently that's not good for cats. Or the mum's blood pressure.

Sebastian was an ignormous wolfhound-cross doggy wot did have some serious actual problems with hoomans but not with cats. He was one very screwed up and confuddled dog! After a very actual bit, the mum and the dad here did persuade Sebastian that not every hooman was going to smack him over the head and he did stop and fink A BIT before trying to eat peoples. Then he did stop and fink A LOT before snapping, till finally he did not really ever want to eat peoples at all. Trouble was, peoples hadn't noticed when Sebastian was frightened. There was Sebastian yawning and turning his head and showing the whites of this eyes, like all dogs do know is how you say 'I is frightened, back off' but because he had actual been hignored, he stopped doing them. And just did snap instead. That did get the stoopid people's attention but it did also get Sebastian kicked out of his house.

The mum and the dad here did teach Sebastian that if he did his signals, then he would be actual hunderstood so he did start doing them again. Mum says Sebastian did land right on his feet when he was dopped. Now he lives in a fuge house with horses and goes to the South of France every actual year on his hollibobs.

The dad is the only person who uses the words Foster

Dog here at the moment. I do not actual know why. When the dad do say to people I are the latest foster, the mum does very actual change the subject. But when peoples do say I are booful and luffly boykin she do smile and give me pats and scratches and take sneaky glances at the dad. The dad hasn't noticed this yet and I don't fink the mum knows that I have. But I has...

29 January 2014

At flipping blinking last. With knobs on. I has FINALLY been allowed to meet the other doggies wot do live very near here. And do you know wot is very actual quite exerlent? They is great! To be very actual honest they coulda been a bit average and boring so long as they weren't cats. But they is not; they is fabumazing.

There is two of them but they is both really little. I reckon you could fit 6 of both of them into one of me. One is a growed up lady terrier. She is about the same size as a hamster. But oh my very actual word, is she a bossy hamster. The mum do say her name is Pip and that I might as well get used to the fact that Pip is in charge. Sebastian, even though he was actual 30 inches tall, did get very quite told off by Pip and did do lying on his back cowering when he did try to be cheeky with her. He never did do THAT again. Mum says I should let Sebastian be a good example or a terrible warning and be ever so very actual quite respectful to Pip. If I do this, then Pip is a noisy, feisty, full of fun play friend. I has decided to do respectful.

The other doggy is called Merlin and he is a puppy Lurcher just like me. Well, his birth mum was a long tall lady Lurcher so he must be a Lurcher, mustn't he? Fing is... he is a bit well, er, short. His daddy was probabbly a guinea pig. Or a basset hound. Or maybe a cross between the two; I are not sure. But apart from being short, Merlin do have all the important other bits of being a Lurcher. He has a fuge long tail and he do like to run and chase and play bitey-facey. We did get on really, wheely well so we are going to be doing lots of playing and walking together. As far as I are concerned, fings could not be any betterer!

30 January 2014

The mum has been out a very lot recently in the evening because she has been doing a Panty Mine. I do not know wot this is but the mum do come back very actual tired but not able to go to sleep for ages afterwards because she says she is all hexcited. She says me and Panty Mine would not get along as it involves lots of singing and dancing and shouting. This do mean that me and the dad has been spending a lot of quality time together doing boy fings like eating a lot of chips. It is a well known fact in this house that Daddy Chips are the best in the actual world. Do not be telling the Mum but I has been sampling quite a very few of them. We has also been watching the football on the telly and shouting at the men running around who are useless and couldn't hit a barn door.

The dad do support Leeds football club which according to him is a fankless task. The mum says she does lots of tasks which no-one says fanks for or even notice except when she don't do them and could he please stack the dishwasher as she is quite actual very tired doing Panty Mine. The dad says he is bonding with me so he can't do housework but this is a very actual rotten trick to play on the mum because she don't have an answer to that. She do want me and the dad to do the bonding quite a very lot. Bonding, it seems, is another word for lying on the sofa doing a very lot of nuffink and is actual quite to my liking.

31 January 2014

Last night, there was a conversation. This is when the mum does a lot of talking at the dad, and the dad stops clicking Uff for long enough to listen to wot the mum has to say. The actual deal is that when he has done saying yes to the mum, he can click Uff again.

The whole actual point of the conversation was me, Worzel Wooface. The mum did want to know from the dad whether they could dop me. The dad did do listening to the mum and did trying quite hard not to laugh. The mum did do lots of talking about me being a luffly boykin and kind to the cats. She did say I do coming back on walks very quite always and she did also show the dad her bum. Happarently the mum's bum is actual getting smaller since I did arrive because she has been doing lots of walking. The mum fort this might be a good hargument to do with the dad. Hoomans are a bit bonkers like that. The dad doesn't actual care wot size the mum's bum is so long as she can fit in her clothes and he doesn't have to go shopping.

Wot the mum doesn't know is that when she was doing Panty Mine, the dad and me did epic bonding. We went for walks down at the harbour to look at the dad's boat and the clanging and flapping of fings did not worry me a-very-tall. These were very slow actual walks because as we did stroll along, I did see lots of peoples I wanted to say hello to. I do particularly like to say hello to other doggies and also to pretty ladies. The dad do say that I do have exerlent taste in women. All the pretty ladies wanted to talk to the dad about me and he did say he was very actual proud of me. He finks that if ever the mum do get very annoyed with him then he wants custardly of me cos that way he'll be able to get another mum. Happarently, you can't have custardly unless you've dopped a dog so he had very quite decided a few days ago that he wanted to dop me but he forted it would be fun see wot the mum would say to get him to say yes.

So, I is going to stay here forever and hever. I has been dopped and everyone is quite very actual frilled to bits bout this. Even me. The peoples here are a bit weird but they do all seem to like each other a lot and a very lot. The mum says I shouldn't be worrying about custardly battles. The dad and the mum have been muddling along for a very actual long time and anyway, the boat is in her name so the dad isn't going anywhere. And neither is I.

FEBRUARY

1 February 2014

Because I has now been dopped, I has got to very get used to calling peoples by their proper actual names. So, I is not calling Mum, 'the mum' anymore and I is not calling Dad, 'the dad' any more neither. From very now on, I shall be calling them 'Mum' and 'Dad'. You might not fink this is himportant but it is to me. There is a fuge actual difference between being 'the mum' and Mum. You do ask anyboddedy.

The previously ginger one and the fuge ginger boyman say they are happy to carry on being called these names in my stories even though I is now dopped and they do both have very actual good real names. They did both say that being identified by their real names might make it hard for them to get a date. Or a job. Or ever live it down. Dad says being a teenager is quite very actual harder than being a luffly boykin doggy.

Being dopped is very different to being fostered. When you is a foster dog you is in training for your real forever famberly so you can make mistakes and the foster mums and dads do help you not be making those mistakes again. The foster mums and dads do talk about the best way to train you and hencourage you to do fings right or not be scared of somefings.

It will be a very long time before I is not scared of somefings and Mum has made me promises that she and Dad did know this before they dopped me. She does say that the himportant fings like not scaring the cats and being a luffly gentle boykin that do make everyone laugh and happy is all there and we will be 'working on the other stuff' as we go along.

So today I did eat a fuge hole in the middle of the new carpet to see how that 'working on the other stuff' would go. It wented ok. Mum says I are still dopped but she has covered the fuge hole with a rug until after Dad has had a cuppatea, his dinner and clicked on Uff for a bit.

2 February 2014

Dad has putted a stair-gate across the sitting room door so I don't be tempted to eat any more carpet. I do fink this is a good idea because it didn't actual taste nice and it has also gived me a bit of a runny bum.

The fuge ginger boyman did say somefing about horses and stable doors and bolts but there do be no horses here so I is a bit confuddled. Sometimes the previously ginger one calls me a donkey, especially if I do step on her feets so maybe that is wot they do mean.

Mum has tooked the blame for the carpet. Happarently, if you dop a dog then you is responsible for everyfing it does do, so it is her fault. She says that because she has been poorly-sick with a sore throat after Panty Mine, I did not get my 'hello-Merlin-your-bum-do-smell-nice-of-wot-you-had-for-tea' and run and play yesterday like I do need every day, so I was bored and that it why I did do it.

The fuge ginger boyman did take me out when he got back from school and he and I is coming to a hunderstanding. He is a bit very actual upset about me being dopped because a few months ago, there was a foster puppy here wot he was very actual fond of. He did want to dop that puppy but Mum said no. He was a luffly puppy but not right for our famberly, Mum says, and as the fuge ginger boyman is nearly actual growed up and will be leaving home quite very soon, his vote didn't count as much as everyboddedy else's.

But when we wented for a walk today, the fuge ginger boyman did talk to me about a Girl He Do Like. I did very exerlent listening and waggy-tailed interested. The fuge ginger boyman said that when he did show the Girl He Do Like a picture of me, Worzel Wooface she was actual quite hinterested and did say I was gorgeous. Which I is.

The fuge ginger boyman loves mud so we did do some very actual fabumazing puddle jumping and wented home all wet and smelly. We did both feel betterer and I do fink that the fuge ginger boyman has done starting to happreciate me a bit very more. The fuge ginger boyman says he will bring the Girl He Do Like over to meet me very quite soon.

4 February 2014

Yesterday I did meet the fuge ginger boyman's Girl He Do Like and I can say I do actual quite approve. It is now all fishal-like that they is acupple. Acuppling is when Hoomans do decide they is not going to be doing snogging with anyone else. Hoomans do take a long time to decide if they is going to be acupple and I do not know why. The fuge ginger boyman says they has been acupple probabbly since the end of December. How does he not know? It is very actual quite strange to me. Dogs are much very different. I did take 5 seconds for me and Merlin to decide that we was going to be best friends forever.

The fuge ginger boyman's Girl He Do Like is called Fizzy which is almost quite true but as she is a teenager Dad says I should be protecting the innersent, as she might be getting fed up with the fuge ginger boyman heventually and want to forget she did ever have anyfink to do with him. Dad do say he wouldn't be actual surprised if this happened. He says the fuge ginger boyman is grubby and has too much hair and never brushes his teeth. Fizzy, Dad says, is flipping gorgeous and booful and what-the-hell does-she-see-in-him. He did want to say more about Fizzy but then he did see the LOOK Mum gave him and did shut up very actual quite quickly. Dad is making his own dinner tonight.

Dogs do not do getting fed up of each other. Once dogs have decided they like each other, they does not do this 'going off each other' fing. Very sometimes, a doggy will be too rough and there will be a short hargument but then they is all back to normal being best friends again. It is all very quite much easier being a dog. Being a hooman must be hard blinking work.

Fizzy is fabumazing because she has somefing called Aspergers. This does make life very easy for me. She do say wot she like and feel wot she feel and does not get involved in all metafors or anyfink complercated like that. Sometimes, she finds all the talking hoomans do too very actual much, so she do come and hang out with me and process wot everyone has said or everyfing she has felt. I do do this as well. I do go to my crate and have an opt-out-quiet-time by my own self. When she is at our house she do sit on the floor and call me a luffly boykin and stroke my ears to do her processing. Me and Fizzy do have a hunderstanding and it is all very quite actual simple; I like her, she do like me and that is very actual quite that. I wish more hoomans were like Fizzy. She do not make atmossfears and she do not like them either, just like me.

I do hope Fizzy and the fuge ginger boyman are going to be acupple for a long time and that Dad is wrong about Fizzy being too good for the fuge ginger boyman. The fuge ginger boyman is actual quite very nice and this morning he did even clean his teeth.

<u>5th February 2014</u>

One fing wented wrong when Fizzy did visit us and it wasn't very me. Mouse the cat is in actual trouble because she did do a poo behind the sofa when Fizzy and the fuge ginger boyman was sitting on it being acupple. This was quite very hembarrassing for the hoomans but Mouse did not care to be actual honest. I did offer very kindly to help clear up but Mum said I was disgustering and shutted the stair-gate on me.

I fink I should tell the story about Mouse a bit betterer because she is actual famous round here. Mum says that being famous does not give her the right to poo behind the sofa though and Fings. Will. Have. To. Change. So this is Mouse's story wot did make her famous.

Once-a-very-pon-a-time, there was a cat, called Mouse. Mouse came to live with Mum and Dad when she was only 5 weeks old because her cat mum was very poorly sick and ranned out of henergy.

Mouse was a real baby and did live in Mum's pocket for a long time to keep her warm. She was very soppy and cuddly (and sucked at Mum's clothes which is a bit very quite not right in the head to be actual honest) and Mum luffed her very, very much.

Then one very day, Mouse did disappear. She did not come in for her breakfast or her dinner or her breakfast or her dinner... and Mum was so sad she did crying. Other cats died in the famberly but they were always said goodbye to nicely but Mouse was not found and Mum always worried and was sad because she did not know wot had happened to her.

In Hamerica they do call this 'closure' and until Mum losted Mouse, she did fink this was tosh. She do not be finking this now...

For five very quite long years, Mum worried and did cry sometimes when she fort of Mouse. Dad was kind and did not tell Mum to get over it which is quite surprising because Dad can be a bit pull-yourself-together. But he did hunderstand, just like Mum did when Dad cried in the cinema watching Finding Nemo... But then one day, hexactly 5 years after she did go missing, Mum did see a picture on her confuser and she did nearly do passing out and being sick. It was Mouse. A very poorly, sick Mouse but definitely Mouse, in a hanimal Opital only one very actual mile from here. Mum managed to remember to be sensible (which was quite a very effort) and did go to double check it was Mouse but it actual really very was.

On 18th December, just before I did come to live here, Mum did get the bestest Christmas present ever, HEVER. Mum and Dad do call it a miracle because they did really believe they was never going to see Mouse again. Mouse did have to stay hindoors getting betterer. She did have to sleep in a crate at night till she did put on weight and not be poorly-sick. Mouse was not actual happy about this at first. But now, no-one can get Mouse to go outside at all. All she does is sit on top of the DVD player.

If I had been missing for five years, I do fink I would have chosen a betterer place but cats can be quite daft sometimes, especially in this house. It do seem that instead of using her tray for weesandpoos, she has taken to going behind the sofa. All the hoomans do agree that this is not ok and also that litter trays are horrid. I do not have a problem with litter trays but the previously ginger one has made it really, wheely, get-away-from-me-you-poo-eating-arggh-don't-lick-me, clear that me not having a problem with litter trays is a massive problem for her.

So today, Mouse was hejected and made to go outside. Mum did not have a nice morning. She sat and panicked and phoned Dad and played on her confuser and had to give herself lots of talking tos. I was also not allowed into the garden in case I did decide to chase Mouse and make her do bogging off for another five years. Mum did cave in after about an hour and Mouse is now back inside sittering on top of the DVD player.

I do hope Mouse is going to get the idea very actual soon because I don't actual fink Dad likes being phoned at work every 10 minutes to give Mum pep talks.

6 February 2014

Just to add to Mum's wobbles and worries at the moment, the fuge ginger boyman is trying to get into Universally. As well as trying to persuade Mouse to go outside yesterday, Mum did also have to worry about the fuge ginger boyman because he did have a hinterview at the Universally he really, wheely wants to go to. He did have to wear very actual smart clothes. Do not be telling anyone but Mum did find his smart clothes in a jumble sale. They did cost a pound. The fuge ginger boyman finks this is very quite actual funny and cool. The previously ginger one finks everyone should have gone to a posh shop and spended all their moneys but Dad says that's because she wanted to go to a posh shop and have the same moneys spended on her. So Dad gave her a pound. She was not actual pleased.

On the way home from his hinterview, all the trains did stop working because of a bon-scare. Turns out there wasn't a bon but it did make getting home quite actual difficult. Mum reckons the fuge ginger boyman should definitely get to go to Universally because travelling across London and home to Suffolk when there is a bon-scare shows how clever and hintelligent he is and it was 'no mean feet.' I do not fink the fuge ginger boyman's feet are mean but everyboddedy here actual finks they is very, very actual nasty. If having actual mean, nasty feet is wot you need to get into Universally, then the fuge ginger boyman will get in no problem at all.

8 February 2014

Today was a Very HIMPORTANT Day. Today I wented aboard our boat and happarently it was very himportant that I liked this. Everyone else was quite very nervous and hexcited about this but I don't know why.

The Biggest Deal was getting me off and on the boat and whether I would co-operate. I cannot do jumping on and off the boat and noboddedy wants me to do this. I are rubbish at jumping to be actual honest so that suits me as very well. Dad did want me and him to have lots of goes at getting on and off the boat so as well as doing getting onto the boat that was floating, we also did gettering on and off one on legs, up a ladder, just in case there was hever an hemergency.

Dad put me over his back with my all 4 very legs danglering down over his chest. And then we did practice going up and down the ladder. I was fabumazing at this and so was Dad. Mum was rubbish. She did stand at the bottom of the ladder squealing 'Please be careful. Please don't drop him,' until Dad did one of his very quite rare Management moments and told Mum to shut the very up. Mum doesn't like ladders or going up high which probabbly explains why she stooded at the bottom having hystericals. But when Dad and me did decide to stay up the ladder on the boat on legs, Mum was forced to come up as well and when she did start to whine about this, Dad did give her a lecture about him carrying a 40 pound dog up and neither of them had died or moaned about it, so could she just hurry up the ladder and put the kettle on.

I was very pleased with myself and enjoyed everyfing. I was so pleased I got over-hexcited and managed to wriggle off down the pub. Dad laughed and said this was typical. Mum just flapped at Dad about me being rubbish at coming back when I was hexcited and could Dad please hold onto the lead a bit better. I did not know about this until a bit later cos I was in the pub...

10th February 2014

Last night there was a right kerfuffle here because Mouse could not be found. I do not fink Mouse likes her name. She never comes when she is called and she very actual didn't yesterday. Maybe she doesn't like being called after somefing she could eat so that's why she hignores everyboddedy when they do yell.

When it gotted to midnight and Mouse still had not

come in, Mum did start to panic. Dad said, 'she managed to look after herself for 5 years perfectly well,' and 'shut that flipping back door, it's freezing!' That did not go down well and Mum Gived. Him. A. Look. So he got a torch and wented outside in the cold for a long time and finally found Mouse hiding under the car about 5 metres from the house.

Dad was not very actual amused but Mum was pleased and I is sure the whole neighbourhood did sigh with very relief. I do fink everyone round knows we have a cat called Mouse now. Apart from Mouse.

11th February 2014

Everyboddedy is quite very actual happy and proud here today because the fuge ginger boyman has gotted a place at the Universally he does really want to go to. His feet must have been actual mean and nasty enough which is fabumazing. Happarently he do need some Hay Levels as well as mean feet so he is now going to have to work on bits of paper even more than he was before. Fizzy is doing very actual well at being pleased for the fuge ginger boyman but if he do get his Hay Levels he will be going to live somewhere a long way away. I don't fink I will like this very actual much and Fizzy isn't too happy about it neither. But we has both decidered to be brave because we do luffs him very much and do want him to do well and be happy.

12th February 2014

I did find one of my old toys in the garden this morning and it is freaking everyboddedy out. It's my rat. When it was very new it didn't look very much like a rat but now that I have played with it and chucked it round and tried to dead it and after I did leave it in the garden for a few days, it has now started to look more and more like a real rat. Happarently this is not good. I did leave it in the bathroom this morning and when Dad did see it he did be doing manly screams. That isn't actual quite true; Dad did squeal like a furious piglet but he says if I don't stop making him look like a plonker in my stories he'll tell Mum to go and get a proper job so she can't be my sektary. One minute he was having a fortful sitting down moment (you know, that moment everyboddedy has in the morning) and the next fing he was making ear-splitting squeaks and hollering. Dad do never, hever be making loud noises so everyboddedy did go running upstairs finking he was having an art attack. Except me. I did do running in the other direction and hid in my crate because I was actual very scared. I was quite shocked and forted I must have done somefing quite very bad and wrong. When Mum did realise that Dad wasn't having an art attack and told him off for frightening luffly Wooface, she did start to actual giggle.

Dad wented off to work in a grump, muttering and scowling that there were plenty of other toys Mum could have got Woo that 'Don't look like beeping rats and this had better not end up on Facebook' and 'Could everyone stop giggling and grow up,' and also 'the kids are old enough to blinking leave home which they will be doing if they don't stop laughing.' He wasn't happy.

I did decide to be helpful at this very point and I did remove my toy rat from the discussion and lefted it safely on the landing.

Which was all very actual good until a couple of hours later, Mum was carrying an ignormous pile of washing up the stairs and she was very finking hard about wot to have for dinner and wondering if the fuge ginger boyman had eated all the eggs hagain and...

After she had frowed all the shirts and jumpers down the stairs and then collected them all up again, and folded them, and removed some socks from my water bowl and dunned starting to breathe normal like, she did decide that ENOUGH was ENOUGH and my rat has been frowed away. I has gotted another toy now. It's a kind of green monster fing wot will never look like a rat no matter how hard it tries.

14 February 2014

Today is Valentine's Day and everyboddedy does know that my bestest Valentine is Merlin. Merlin gets teased about being the shortest Lurcher in the whole wide world but I don't care; I luffs him. Luffing isn't about wot you look like; it is all about actions speaking louderer than words.

Fizzy is definitely liking the fuge ginger boyman's actions today. They has had a special meal wot he did cook by himself. Mum is glad that he did do this at Fizzy's house though because although the fuge ginger boyman is a fabumazing cook, he is very actual quite hawful at clearing up afterwards. Mum says he is having a compertition with himself to see how many pots and pans he can use and he finks he has failed if he hasn't used every single blinking one of them.

The previously ginger one doesn't have a boyfriend. She is very off boys at the moment but Mum says that won't last. Dad says he is quite glad she doesn't have a boyfriend because he can never get in the bathroom as it is and yet another teenager hanging around would mean he'd end up having to pee in the garden like Worzel Wooface. I don't see wot's wrong with pee-ing in the garden to be actual honest. In very fact, if I do pee hindoors it do cause quite an actual kerfuffle. It has only happened a few times but noboddedy was actual himpressed and Mum did make a funny quick shocked Woo noise which did make me feel very odd. She did not be doing shouting or telling me off but there was very quite somefing in her voice that did make me fink it wasn't the right very actual fing to do.

The previously ginger one says Dad must not do wee-ing in the garden; someone might see him and fink our famberly is even weirder than they already do. Mum says if he's going to pee in the garden, please can he go in the compost bin cos the man off Gardener's World says this is a good fing to do. The previously ginger one says she is never going to bring a boyfriend to our house, HEVER.

15 February 2014

During the night, One of our fences wented for a dance and then dropped down dead in the middle of the garden. Dad says dancing does this to you which is why he's never doing it. I did have an hexplore but there is another fence behind the one that is now in bits in the flower beds so I can't be going for a wander. It's very actual quite hinteresting to see wot's up the lane in that direction though. I has spent a long time today looking up the lane, making Mum panic that she has missed a gap and that I are going to bog off.

It was really windy here earlier and we're not even getting a mention by the news man on the telly so it must be really bad in other places. Happarently, the rest of the United Kingdom is under water or under snow or getting blown off the map. Mum says that Somerset, where I did used to live, is hunder water and peoples down there are very quite cross about it. I do fink that if my house was soggy or drowned I would be very quite angry too. Dad says we are getting off lightly. It doesn't feel like it to be actual honest. It is very quite noisy and windy and actual scary because everyboddedy is screwing up their faces and yelling to be heard which makes them look cross and angry, although they do keep saying they are not.

When the wind gets up my bum I are very silly and naughty and there is 'fat chance of me coming back' so we waited until the wind stopped blowing-a-hooley to go for our walk. The woods were very not a good idea because we didn't want any wobbly trees landing on our head so we wented up to the best field in the world. It was all boggy and squishy and just perfick for running about in. It even has a paddling pool in the middle of it. I did end up looking like I was wearing stockings because the mud was actual black and sticky. Louise and Mum did laughing at me so I did decide to shake all the smelly, black bog mud all over them. Then they did swearing instead.

18 February 2014

Today we has had some news about sailing habroad with dogs. Habroad is where people eat yummy food and don't speak English. We found out from the guv'ment wot the actual rules are. The rules say that I do need a pet passport and a microchip and lots of injections to make sure I are safe. That bit makes actual very sense.

The rest of it is a load of tosh, according to Dad, and isn't going to keep anyone safe or stop anyone from being ill-eagle or breaking the rules. I can leave the UK on our boat but when I come back, I have to go on an approved route by ferry. At first we fort I might have to travel both ways on a ferry which according to Dad is beyond boring, so finding out I only have to go one way is betterer than nuffink but it's all a bit bonkers. I could sail to France and then to Ireland and then I could come back on our little boat because there are no restrictions between Ireland and the UK. So if someone wanted to do somefing ill-eagle or get round the rules, then it is quite actual possible. Dad says the law is a donkey but we will be doing the law because the fort of me getting stuck in jail is not worth the risk.

I was really, wheely hoping I could be called Captain Worzel on our boat but Dad says the position of Captain is already filled so I will have to be Seadog Worzel. He says he'll decide whether I are a Nable or Unable Seadog when I've been on the boat when it's actual very moving.

21 February 2014

Every Friday, Mum's great friend Vera does come round to help me with interior design. This is wot you call it when you put stuff in places where no-one can find it and get rid of all the field and pond and puddles I have dragged back from my walks. I very like the interior designing day, especially when my bed does get shaken out and all the fings I have collected during the week are tutted about and gived back to their rightful owner. Everyfing does get taken out of the crate and it is like getting presents. I do often find a fing that I have forgotted about and get very actual pleased to see it again. Sometimes there is somefing really, wheely special in my crate wot Vera refuses to touch and she yells at Mum to come and Deal. With. It. This is usually a dead mouse wot the cats have broughted me in as a late night takeaway. If they do bring them in during the day, Mum does snatch them away but Gipsy will often leave one lying about during the night. Then it is just a case of gettering it into my crate before Mum notices.

Of all the cats here, Vera likes Frank best but she is not allowed to feed him because Mum says he is a bulimic nutcase and so fat he can barely squeeze through the cat-flap. So, Vera and Frank spend a lot of time talking about this in the kitchen. Don't tell anyone but I know Vera sneaks Frank some food when Mum isn't looking.

Me and Vera have very different ideas about wot we want to hachieve but we get on quite very well. Vera likes to pick fings up and I like to scatter them around. I like to chew magazines up and she says this isn't very helpful. I fink Vera will like me even more betterer if I stop eating the carpet but she doesn't get cross or anyfink, she just tuts. A lot.

When Vera has a big pile of stuff on the floor, I like to check through the pile to make sure she isn't throwing anyfink away that is important. Vera and I do often not agree about wot is rubbish and wot is for keeping. She do get confuddled about half deaded bones wot I are saving for a quiet day and puts them in the throwing away pile. I do get them out again. Vera would like to tell me to stop doing this but she can't because it makes her go all mushy cos it reminds her of Charlie, the previous famberly dog.

There are pictures here of Charlie. He was a big black and white collie cross. He was very, very naughty and a 'scape artist. He could get over almost any fence or hedge and heven though he did know it was actual not allowed, he did regularly leave the garden for a wander. When he was younger he did like to jump over the fence and chase people riding bikes down the lane. His favourite type of bike person was those men who look like they've jumped out of superhero magazines, wearing glow in the dark tights that give you a very lot of too much information about wot's going on in their pants. Mum used to try to get them to stop peddling because once they did, Charlie would lose interest and come back home. But if they did not hear her or if they was scared by Charlie and peddled faster and faster, Charlie used to fink it was a fabumazing game and just keep going... and going. One time, Mum had to drive after Charlie and one of the men with orange tights and too much trouser information because he would not stop peddling and Charlie was halfway to the seaside.

23 February 2014

At night, Mum likes to go up to bed early and read. She says I can go into the bedroom to say hello and have a cuddle if I very like to. Dad says this is ok too but I are not allowed to fall asleep on the bed and then have a hissy fit when he wants me to go downstairs. A few times I has been very deeply asleep and dunned refusing to wake up and he has had to heject me to go into the garden for weesandpoos and I has had a bit of a grumble about it. This is very not acceptababble.

But at the moment Mouse will not let me into the bedroom. She used to be actual alright with me but as she has got betterer she has decided to be more very hassertive. I wish she would find someboddedy else to hassert herself with. Last night, I wented in to see Mum and mean, nasty hoity-toity Mouse hissed at me and frightened me. I ranned away. When I fort the coast was clear and I did decide to try again, she sprang up and ran across the bed and hissed and spat and made herself look like a puffy ninja hellcat and chased me down the stairs. I are sure it is in the rules somewhere that dogs are actual supposed to chase cats, not the other way round. I do fink it is not fair that dogs in foster get checked that they are cat safe but no-one do actual check if the cats are dog safe. Mouse is currently not dog safe. She is being mean and I is hupset.

24 February 2014

There is one little fing that Mum is rubbish at with dogs. She does not like to cut their toe nails. Mum started off quite ok at it but Charlie had black nails and he did not make it easy for anyboddedy.

Over the years he got more cross about it and Mum got more useless at it and round and round it wented until Mum gived up and got Vanessa to cut his nails because Vanessa is a proper trained dog groomer and did not be having hystericals. Vanessa did not mind doing this nor did she do laughing at Mum for being pathetic because she also forted Charlie was hawful when it came to nail clippering. Even when he was actual 15 years old, he did do trying to eat Vanessa's hand when she was cutting his nails. He didn't have many teeth left so it didn't hurt and to be very honest, everyone was quite actual himpressed he did still have that much energy in him. You can get away with all sorts when you are ancient it would very seem. Anyway, after Charlie, Mum has always been scared and wobbly about it but she did decide that she had to be getting over it with me and stop being reedickerless.

I could tell Mum was actual nervous when she did join me on the landing. She was trying to be cheerful (wot do never fool Worzel Wooface) but I did let her having a little clippy nibble on each foot so she would not feel like a complete actual very failure. Then I kindly wented and hid in my crate. I could tell Mum had had a-very-nuff and needed to go and lie down with some wine.

I are hoping she is going to give up being brave and responsibabble about my nails and let someone do it who doesn't need actual ferapy afterwards. I can't see me having many toes left at this rate.

25 February 2014

Today, Mum had to take the previously ginger one to an Opital to make sure her ears work properly so I has entered the world of work!

I do not like Dad's car; it is too small and a bit like a go-cart and I cannot look out of the window and have my seat belt on at the same time. But when we got there is was very, very actual quite hexciting.

At the boatyard where Dad does work, dogs are welcome and lots do go with their Mums and Dads. There are 3 black mostly Labradors and 2 terrier muddles. I was actual very hexcited to see everyone. The terrier muddles are quite very hassertive, especially Buffy who do fink he owns all the boat shed. The boat shed is about the size as a football field so that is a very actual lot of owning to fink! Dad did take my bed and my longest lead and I did lie down on it when he was using his workbench but then he did do trying to go to a different place outside to fix a boat. I was having none of very it. I did fink I was going to be left forever. First I did concerned woofing. Then I did 'Come back here you horrible Dad' barking. Then I did 'I'm sooo gonna tell Mum on you yelling.' Then I fort, stuff it, chewed through the lead and wented after him. Dad says he was goned for no more than 3 minutes but I do fink he was gone at least 17 years.

After that I was promoted to management and got to be in the office with the mostly Labradors which was much, much more very fun. We did playing and shouting and causing lots of very actual chaos.

I are allowed to go back again because Worzel Wooface is a friendly boykin but we will not make it an everyday fing because I are still very young and have lots of playing and learning to do. Dad says he won't have me out in the yard with him until I can let him actual do some work but I fink I prefer the office. There is a sofa and play friends. Who wants to do proper work when you can be a Manager?

<u>28 February 2014</u>

Because I have been here for more than an actual month now, Mum finks it's about time we got betterer at training. Training is fings like 'wait' and 'come' and 'off' and 'sit.'

Now, there is some fings about training I do not actual fink is a bad idea. 'Wait' is ok. That is when I stop doing wot I is doing. So, we might use 'Wait' if I has gotted too far ahead of everyboddedy else and they is panting to keep up, or it might be that Mum needs to go through a door first to make sure there aren't any monsters in the next room.

'Come,' Mum says, is pretty blinking essential. 'Come' is wot I should do when we is out and she wants me to go back on a lead, or stop heading for a muddy ditch, or not notice the pheasant that is about to fly out of the hedge. I can do 'come' very actual quite well usually but sometimes I do pretend to be deaf. Mum says I have political hearing; I do hear wot I want to hear and she would not be that actual far wrong.

If Mum is stoopid enough to say 'come' in the house then I always very bog off. I learned before I was rescued when I was a baby that 'come' when I are hindoors means I have either done somefing actual bad and wrong or that somefing strange or odd or fiddling about with me is going to happen. So I do go and hide in my crate.

Sit. I blinking HATE Sit. Yes I can do it if I habsolutely very have to, but 'sit' is not easy when you is shaped like a horse. Have you ever seen a horse doing 'sit?' Well, sitting comes as naturally to me as it does to a pony. And everyboddedy do expect me to 'sit' on a hard floor or gravel. If you is a boy, you will hunderstand that pressing your gentleman bits onto a cold floor or prickly stones is very actual painful and wrong. But I can earn very lots of brownie points doing 'sit' so I suffer it very sometimes. I do hope Mum happreciates all this actual effort I do go to for her.

I can do 'off' but I do sulk about it. 'Off' means get off the sofa or the bed which I would rather not do because they is comfy but if I does not get 'off' then people do sometimes shove up or squish me until I do get the message and then I do HAVE to get 'off.' Or fall off.

You might be actual wondering if Mum does positive reward based training. Mum would LOVE to do positive reward based training. Trouble is, Worzel Wooface aren't falling for them tricks. Not on your blinking actual Nelly.

There is no food tasty enough or hinteresting enough that will persuade me to just blindly do wot Mum wants me to do. I maybe only 6 months old but I learned the hard way. Treats are tricks wot get you into trouble. Offer me a treat and I'm very off. Mum reckons I was beated up for taking food when I was a baby. You want me to eat somefing, put it in my bowl. I know where I are with food in my bowl. It's definitely mine and no-one's going to do actual yelling at me for eating it.

Balls and frowing toys are not my friends neither. Frow a ball and I'll watch you go and pick it up again. A tuggy toy? Forget it. I aren't tugging very nuffink.

So Mum has decidered that seeing as 'normal' dog training isn't going to actual work, she is going to teach me to hunderstand English cos that's wot everyboddedy else uses in this house. So far, I has learnt 'luffly-boykin' and 'hello-Wooface,' and will always be waggy-tails when I do hear this. My latest words are 'get back, you plonker,' when someone do come to the door so Mum can open it without me getting a very actual shock. It's funny; the person on the other side of the door finks they are being protected from me when it's actual the other way round.

Louise, Pip and Merlin's mum, would like me to learn 'slow down' and 'look where you're going' before she ends up with a broken leg. Mum is Sighthound hexperienced so she do be very able to dodge me quite actual well; Louise is getting hexperienced the hard way. The key to havoiding a collision with a fuge Worzel Wooface is to stand like you are balancing on a surf board with your arms out as if you is trying to fly. You has to hope that none of the neighbours are watching because they will fink you are auditioning for the next Mission Impossible film. Then you has to hanticipate when I will be arriving. It is always very actual much sooner than you do fink. The bestest fing is to stand your ground, then bend your knees or twist your hips so that I do brush past you and you do say 'phew.' Your other choice is to decide that I has not seen you and move. Most times I see peoples at the last very minute and do a fabumazing athletic, twisty dodge. Hunfortunately, Louise has not yet got any faith in my twisty dodging skills and jumps out of the way... to the very spot I has decided to aim for in order to havoid her. Then she do find herself on her bum in the mud with me all tangled up in her and Merlin jumping on her head because he do fink it is a great game. I fink Louise is going to learn to stand still much fasterer than I is going to learn to slow down.

So, whilst I is never going to be one of those dogs that does like dancing to music or flyball or hobedience showing off, Mum finks that in time I could become quite user-friendly because I are very attentive to wot she is saying and keen to do the right fing. She would love it if I would take a treat off her without believing I are going to get fumped because she finks my life would be much more fun that way. Pip and Merlin both very like treats so Mum is hoping I do learn by example... heventually.

MARCH

<u>1 March 2014</u>

I wented to somefing called Rugby today. Rugby seems to be a game I could be good at. Basically you run and push and shout and shove each other around and very hoccasionally, you do somefing with a ball. But mainly it seems to be about mud. It's right up my street.

The fuge ginger boyman was doing playing Rugby. He has been playing with the same group of boymen for a long time and they do know each other actual quite well. This I did fink was actual himportant because after about 10 minutes, they looked nearly actual hidentical because of all the mud.

Lots of dogs did watch the Rugby and I did need to say 'hello-who-are-you-I-are-luffly-Worzel-boykin' to all of them. It was very actual quite hard work for the hoomans because all the dogs did have the same idea as me, so untangling us all was very difficult. Happarently, we are betterer at doing knitting than watching Rugby.

None of us dogs was allowed to join in with the Rugby. I do not fink is actual fair because we would have been fabumazing at it. It is hexactly like a game of zoomie bitey-facey for hoomans. Believe it or not we were not allowed to play because of somefing called The Rules.

At Rugby, instead of a mum or dad or a senior dog like

Pip yelling 'Oy! That's enough now,' there is a man with a whistle who is in charge of The Rules. He do blow his whistle when someboddedy has broken one of The Rules. It seems like all he does do is spoil a very actual quite good game of bitey-facey. You is allowed to give the ball to someone else but you have to do it backwards. If you do it forward the man with the whistle do give the ball to the other team. And the hoomans do let him! This is all in The Rules. Heventually, one of the hoomans will get the ball over a line and score a point. In Rugby it is called a try. I can see actual why; wot the man with his whistle and the mud and The Rules you do have to try blinking hard to score a point.

The man with the whistle does not like it if you shove someone who does not have the ball. I fink this is bonkers crazy but it is in The Rules. Most of the hoomans did not seem to like doing this Rule either because I did see a lot of them doing shoving peoples who did not have the ball, even if the man with the whistle did not.

Mum does not like to be watching the fuge ginger boyman play Rugby. Once he did dislocate his shoulder doing it and every time he do play it goes wonky again. He has himportant hexams this year and cannot be getting broken and not being able to write, Mum says. Lots of the boymen in the team have himportant hexams this year because they are all the same actual age so most of the Mums and Dads are worried about their boymen getting hinjured. So, I has come up with a cunning plan. I do actual fink that next time, us dogs should do the Rugby, the boys should do the knitting wot is safe and the man with the whistle and his poxy Rules should stay in bed so he doesn't spoil our game.

3 March 2014

I met some Very Himportant Dogs today. I met Tilly and Dezzie who were the first ever foster dogs Mum and Dad did have. Tilly and Dezzie were strays and when they did live here they knew nuffink; they didn't even know how stairs worked. Mum and Dad had to show them; it took Tilly ages to work it out and she used to get stuck at the top, too scared to come down.

Tilly had been used as a hunting dog and had been dumped when she got no good at it. When she first did arrive she kepted rubbing her nose because it was driving her hinsane. She had a hoperation and they did find out that the fing making her nose itch was some teeth from a fox wot had gotted stucked right into her bones. This was horrible for actual Tilly but I do fink it can't have been much very fun for the fox neither.

When strays do come into foster, you does not very often know wot they has been up to and wot they can do. One night Dad tooked Tilly and Dezzie for a walk and when Dad did turn on a torch, Tilly did turn into a different dog. She'd done somefing called lamping and she was very, very quite hinterested in following the torch light. She did run off so blinking fast she did snap the lead right off and was belting around like a very actual maniac. Because Dad knew nuffink a-very-tall about lamping and hunting and all that stuff... and he don't actual want to, to be quite very honest, he did decide to turn off the torch before him and Tilly did get into any troubles.

Where we do live there is no street lights and they was in the middle of a wood, in the dark; proper countryside dark. He did do a very lot of stumbling about in the woods, tripping over everyfing, trying to find his way out without using the torch in case Tilly saw somefing and started doing chasing again. When he did heventually get home he did look like a swamp monster and Mum did do a very lot of laughing.

Nowadays, Mum and Dad are a bit more hexperienced and don't be falling for no Sighthounds tricks. Mum says you do get very actual brilliant at looking at the horizon to see fings before a dog can and then getting them back on a lead very actual quite quick. And they don't go out in the dark with a Lurcher and a torch no more neither...

Dad and Mum love Tilly and Dezzie very much. I fink they would have dopped them if Tilly had not wanted to eat all the cats. Now they live with their forever mum and dad quite near to us so my Mum and Dad get to see them which is quite very nice for everyone.

Tilly fort I was fun and liked chasing me. Dezzie fort I was too actual much and kept telling me to go away. This made everyone laugh because Dezzie is a bit of a wimp and just likes showing off to big puppies like me. Tilly, though can be quite a handful so it's a good job I managed to himpress her with my exerlent manners.

5 March 2014

Yesterday I had to have a bath because I did find a ditch with oily, sticky smelly stuff in it. I did suffer this bath because although I don't much like them, the bit afterwards is fabumazing. That's the bit where you get over-hexcited and you shake everywhere, roll on Mum's bed, race madly up and down the stairs and pee on the landing. Mum says before anyone says that's cos I was all stressed; I wasn't. I was being a prat.

6 March 2014

It was a smashing, sunshiny day here yesterday so we did do gardening. I was very quite actual exerlent at it. Mainly, I did the lying about in the sunshine but of gardening I found a new spot to lie in as well, with wonder-actual-ful views and a nice smooth surface far nicerer than gravel. Mum says everyone else calls it a table.

I also did help with making holes. Mum says she is in charge of digging holes in her garden and could I not. Please. Especially not near the purple sprouting broccoli that she has been looking forward to eating since last June wot is nearly ready to pick.

She has finally moved the annoying rose out of my way. I are very pleased about this because I has been trying to get it out of the ground since I did arrive here. It was right in my actual direct path from the back garden to the front gate and ruining my Salt Course. It seems Mum has finally very agreed with me that it needs to be moved before either me or the rose suffer a fatal hinjury.

Mum decided not to tell the fuge ginger boyman about the holes I made. Last time the fuge ginger boyman and Mum talked about holes, it was a long hargument about whether a hole existed or not and whether you can make an absence of somefing. Mum decided she didn't want this tiring conversation again which would only end when Dad said, 'How long is it until he leaves for Uni.'

Universally sounds like fun if they teach you about diggering holes. I fink I need more practice at digging holes in the right place. Everyboddedy else finks I just need to stop doing it.

9 March 2014

I are actual in the dog house. I just wented upstairs to say good morning to Dad and jumped right on top of him. Under the duvet he has somefing called goolies wot he doesn't want stooded on. Specially not when he is fast asleep. Once he did be able to speak and breathe again he said I was a 'blinking great carthorse' and told me to go downstairs.

10 March 2014

My mission to get everyone to clear up is going very actual well. I have so far eated 3 pairs of leather shoes left lying around, chewed 2 pair of wellies I founded by the back door and taken several slippers into the garden. Last night I founded Mum's kindle in her bed so I ate that too. I forted I was going to be in trouble but Dad says he do fink it is everyboddedy else's fault for not putting their fings away. I do fink that every dog should have a Dad like mine because he is always, mainly, usually, hoccasionally very on my side. So long as I aren't jumping on his goolies.

12 March 2014

I wented for a walk with a new friend today. She is called Faye, and she lives with Mum's great friend Anna. Faye is supposed to be a very well trained dog but she is quite naughty when she isn't being well-trained. She did lead me astray and it was fun! She took me into hedges and joined in when I did chase the seagulls off the farmer's fields.

I do not chase many fings and in lots of ways I are a useless Sighthound which is a relief to everyboddedy. I never see the rabbits in the hedges and the one time I did flush out a pheasant, it took off near my head and I did have actual hystericals and hidded behind Mum. But I can't resist a seagull or a crow sitting on a field. I do run off after them and they do ALWAYS fly off just when I are within hinteresting range. It's very almost as if they wait until the last minute when I is getting all quite hopeful and then they do fly off. It is very quite actual frustrating. So I don't feel like a total quite plonker, I do pretend I are doing a great public service for the world by stopping the birds eating the crops. Mum says that me belting around all over the crops might not be considered that helpful.

13 March 2014

Last night when Mum was out, me and Dad had a chat about women and about how complercated they are and how they can lead you astray.

Yesterday Faye was flirty with me. When we got back home, I found myself trying to do Fings To Cushions that I don't really hunderstand. Dad says it's because I are growing up but he also said that I should not do these fings, especially not in plite-comp-knee. So there is no confusion, he says, plite-comp-knee is all the time if it hinvolves me doing Fings To Cushions. Faye has been dunned happarently so there is no danger of me getting into trouble. Dad wouldn't explain wot dunned was or how this works with plite-comp-knee and why I could get into trouble. He says I are not to worry about it and that he definitely isn't going to fink about it or talk about it but mainly could I 'Stop shagging the cushions!'

The other lady in my life is Pip. Pip does not make me want to do Fings To Cushions. Pip does not do flirting a-very-tall. Recently, she has also been trying to lead me astray but not in the same way as Faye.

Sometimes, Pip decides that she has a nagenda. Then, she will wait for people to get a bit far ahead and sneakily turn round and bog off home. We all end up looking for her and chasing after her and then she has to go on a lead to finish the walk.

Yesterday, Pip did decide that we were going to the woods. We had all planned to run and chase along wot we call the bee strip where the farmer has planted lots of wild flowers so that bees come and kiss his crops. It is a very brilliant place for hoomans and dogs to walk and Mum says we are very actual quite lucky to have it. Pip, however, decided that we were going to the woods and waited until our backs were turned and noboddedy was looking and ran as fast as she could, under 2 stiles and stood waiting at the entrance to the wood.

When Pip has a nagenda she can be very actual fast. And tiny. So you don't always see wot she is doing until she's dunned it. I was an exerlent boy and didn't jump the stiles or anyfink but I did want to follow her and Mum had to say my name several times loudly to make sure I did not follow. Being fuge sometimes has its dishadvantages; every blinking move you make is seen for miles.

Everyone agrees that Pip is a little madam and that she is not in charge of everyfing. Especially when it means that she is leading me and Merlin astray.

So, Pip is going to have to be on a lead for walks for a few days until she forgets about being in charge of route-planning. That means that Pip is going to be very bossy and hopinionated and tell everyone wot she finks of the situation. The next few walks could be very extra noisy.

<u>15 March 2014</u>

Today I was allowed to go to out to lunch at a pub. I was a really fabumazing boykin and laid quietly under the table. Mum says she was hunbelievababbly proud of me. I founded one of those super sunny patches on the floor and snoozed while everyone talked and spilled coffee everywhere.

I met Ben, who is Mum's brother. He usually lives in Los Angeles which haccording to the previously ginger one is beyond cool and very hot. Happarently this makes sense.

Ben said I looked like a camel. I fink dogs in Los Angeles must look very strange if Ben finks I look like a camel. Then again, most people in Ingerland don't have orange faces like Ben so maybe fings is different over there.

<u>16 March 2014</u>

Back in January, Mum said she would do a 25 mile walk up the 3 highest peaks in Yorkshire for Charity. Charity must be a very persuasive because Mum is 44, a bit chubby, not very fit and we live in Suffolk where there are no hills to practice on at all. The previously ginger one reckons Mum must have had too many ciders when she said she would do it. Dad reckons it is the most reedickerless fing he has ever heard of and Mum is going to do herself a hinjury.

Pip and Merlin's mum, Louise, is also doing this walk. Louise is actual quite fit and does running and dancing all the very time. She is one of those fitness fantix and she is also fusey-tastic about getting out of breath and making bits of you hurt for the fun of it. Louise is in charge of training which is a good job because Mum would really rather not do training even if it is for Charity.

Today, Mum and Louise wented for their first proper big practice walk. Their plan was to walk 10 whole miles but because I are still not fully growed, I was only allowed to come along for some of it.

When Dad did come to pick me up he was very quite himpressed that Mum was still alive. So was Mum. Louise was bouncing around like a mad fing and Dad reckons she is Haydee Aydee.

They did finish their 10 miles and Mum made it home without any help or doing hinjuring herself. Mum is all oppymistic now but I do fink she has forgotted about the hills.

17 March 2014

Mum couldn't actual move this morning so Dad was in charge. I did some helping in the garden. It was my version of helping again so Dad is in Mum's bad books.

18th March 2014

I wented for a walk with Dad and there were woolly sheep fings in my usual field so I had to go for a longer hadventure. We wented to a big meadow and there was a little version of me with a coat on called Marnie. She was not very pleased to see me. She did chase me and shout at me. You would actual fink it was her own actual private field the way she was yelling and shouting but it very quite isn't. She was with her Dad as well so whilst Marnie tried to get me off-her-land, my Dad and her Dad did have a chat. Marnie's Dad said Marnie is a little madam who finks she owns the hentire world. She can't have metted Pip yet and I actual don't want to be there when it happens.

Wot was really very surprising was that she was as fast as me which was very shocking and hexhausting. I did have to use my 5th gear to keep in front and out of the way of her shouty bits.

When Dad was ready to go home, I did decide I was very not ready and I did the fandango. This is where I do decide I are NOT coming back and I are NOT going back on the lead. I forted I had very won but then Dad did walk off and I fort he was going to leave me with Marnie-who-owns-the-hentire-world, so I had to run to catch up with him. I was in a right very panic. Dad is sneaky like that.

19 March 2014

Mum is in the dog house. Yesterday, we were having cuddles and Mum was doing reading. She wented to stroke me without putting the book down and I did have hystericals and got all confused. I did jump in the air like a harrier jump jet and was quite very upsetted. I fort she was going to bonk me on the nose with the nasty mean book! I did do running away and hiding and would not do talking to Mum at all.

Mum said sorry very nicely. This did mainly involve hignoring me very hard for several hours and waiting until I wanted to come and say hello again. She says this was blinking very heart-breaking because when you are waiting to be forgived, time passes very, very actual slowly.

We are starting to be bestest friends again now but Mum is still muttering to herself. She told Dad that she is a 'stupid idiot who's probably undone 8 weeks work in one stupid unfinking moment.' I do fink she is almost as actual very cross and hupset as I am.

This morning I have eated the book so it can't attack me again. I have noticed that there are lots of other books in this house so I hope they won't be getting any funny ideas as I don't fink I could eat them all.

20 March 2014

Today was very quite hinteresting. First, I wented for a long walk in a direction I have not gone before. There was all sorts of fings to smell and it rained and someone had dropped bread rolls along the route. I did feel like Hansel following the trail but Mum said I was not allowed to eat yucky gluten because it might make my tummy go pop. A big black collie dog came out of his house and stooded in the middle of the road shouting at us. Mum had to slow some traffic down so the cars didn't hit him!

I founded out we were walking to a place called Stoven Hall Equine Clinic to meet someone called Sally-the-Vet. I did seriously fink about doing Complaints to the Management about this because equine means horses and animals like that. I are starting getting an hidentitee crisis. Wot with Ben calling me a camel, and other people calling me a carthorse and the previously ginger one saying I are a donkey, fings are very actual confuddling. I is a luffly boykin Worzel Wooface and I. Are. A. Dog. It's just that my feet are too big for the rest of me.

It turns out that although Sally-the-Vet does mainly look after horses, she will also look after luffly boykins but I was not actual convinced at first. Sally's room did smell very strange and I wasn't at all sure about it or her. Then she did get down on the floor with me to say 'Hello you gorgeous fella, aren't you a wonderful doggy.' I was very actual pleased about this and did decide that as she could tell the very difference between a camel and a Worzel Wooface, we could be friends and she could be my Vet. I did play very hard to get with Sally-the-Vet cos of her smelly room but I are a sucker for people who is nice to me and do not make loud bangs. Also, Sally-the-Vet had all her books under control.

Sally-the-Vet says that I are a growing boy and probabbly won't stop growing for another 9 whole months at least. This explains why my feet are so ignormous and why some people do mistake me for a horse. It is also very good news for my gentleman bits cos both Sally-the-Vet finks that they should stay until I are fully grown both fizzcly and ermotionly.

We did find out two fings which are wrong with me. First of all, my microchip has bogged off. I is an unchipped Worzel. So, Mum will be asking her friend to do me another one quite very soon. This is actual very quite urgent and himportant because if I did get lost, noboddedy would know where I do belong.

And also, there is some gunk in my ears. This is why

I've been putting my paws over my ears. It is not to look cute, like Fizzy and the previously ginger one did fink, it is cos there is somefing in there wot is driving me crackers. I did decide to let Sally-the-Vet put some stuff in my ears because she did know I was not a horse but I do not fink I do want it to happen again. Sally-the-Vet did give the rest of the bottle to Mum so I fink Mum must have gunk in her ears as well.

21 March 2014

Turns out the Sally-the-Vet wanted Mum to stick the rest of the bottle of stuff down MY ears. If Mum finks she is sticking anyfink down my ears she is going to need to come up with a betterer plan.

22 March 2014

I fink Mum has gived up on the ear fing... cos I have made it very quite stonkingly clear that we is going to fall out big time if she doesn't. She's going to phone Sally-the-Vet to see if there is another solution. She does not need to be phoning Sally-the-Vet for another solution; I has got one. Do. Not. Be. Sticking. Anymore. Stuff. Down. My. Ears.

25 March 2014

Today I saw a horse! It was real and everyfing. First of all, me and the horse did waggy greetings and then we did walk all along the fence together. Every time I did take a step, the horse followed me and treated me like a long lost relative. This was very confuddling and did make me feel like I was having an hidentitee crisis again.

I can tell you I does not fink I are a horse and I has hevidence. The horse did eat grass and looked like it very enjoyed it. I only eat grass when there is somefing in my tummy I want to get out in an actual hurry. I watched for ages and the grass very did not come back out of the horse again. Well, not out of the end I was watching.

26 March 2014

Well, I did promise that I would share my disasters as well as my successes. Today, we wented to see a nice lady to get me micro-chipped wot is himportant for my safety and my hollibobs.

I was fine being held still. But as soon as the not-very-nice-lady-after-all did touch me with the machine I did have actual quite very hystericals. I did a massive combination of a toddler wot does not want his seat belt on, a bucking bronco horse (another horse wot I are not related to) and one of those toys that you lick the rubber to the base and then wait for it to suddenly jump up. We tried twice but it was very actual no good. It was an hexplosion of Worzel everywhere.

We did all agree that it was too very Orrendous to try again. I have no padding and if I did knock the hateful-'orrible-not-nice-at-all lady's hand, I could knock the needle into a dangerous place and that might stop my legs working. I are very glad they did decide to actual stop.

Mum finks that someone might have electrocuted me or dunned somefing else nasty to me when I was tiny. I seem to have a real deep fear of long thin fings touching me. We didn't get anywhere near even putting the chip in.

The good news is that I was waggy-tail-friendly-I-forgive-you with Mum and the 'now-you're-not-holding-that-weapon-you're-ok' lady quickly afterwards and I has very quite got over it now. I do fink it is going to take a very actual lot of wine for Mum to get over it though.

29 March 2014

Today has been a quite actual strange and different day. First of all, I had Complaints to the Management cos there was no dinner last night and no breakfast this morning which is not very on.

Then at lunchtime I wented to see Sally-the-Vet and Mum did leave me there which I was not very quite actual happy about until Sally-the-Vet gived me a cuddle and a 'do-you-remember-me-yes-I-do-you-is-gorgeous' rub on my neck with some sticky stuff. Then I wented all whoozy as if I had drunk too many pints of beer like the fuge ginger boyman did do once. Actual very more than once but I is getting away from the very point...

I did spend some time having a snooze and watching Sally-the-Vet doing her paperwork. She did have me right beside her in her office; no kennels for a luffly boykin and I was very treated like an actual VIP. It was all very personal treatment wot like you get in one of those spa private Opital posh places. I shall be calling Sally-the-Vet's place Hotel de Stoven Hall now cos I do get 5 star treatment.

While I was asleep, Sally-the-Vet did give me my jabs and put my microchip in. She also did stick the rest of the stuff down my ears that Mum and I had very actual quite agreed wasn't going to be happening in either of our lifetimes HAND she did also finish cutting my toe nails. So now I are almost ready for my hollibobs, my ears don't itch no more and Mum does not be needing trauma ferapy neither! We are all happy now cos there is a plan in place for any time I do need fixing. It is a bit more actual expensive than the usual way of doing fings but Mum says I are worth it. Dad says could I not break too actual often because he wants to buy some new sails at some point this century.

30 March 2014

Today is Mother's Day and there are too very blinking many of them round here for me to actual cope with. I do feel sorry for the previously ginger one. She is the oldest daughter, of the oldest daughter (Mum) of the oldest daughter (Grannie Annie), of the oldest daughter (Granny Mary) and when they do all get in the same room together the gene pool is really, wheely crowded and she is right at the bottom.

Dad loves it when they all get together. He gets to see

his mother-in-law being treated like an actual 12 year old by her mum which does make him giggle a very lot. He says that is worth all the noise and being shouted at by 4 generations of bossy women. Every time they do get together everyone does remind Mum not to leave the freezer door open. She did do this once 30 years ago and no-one is hever going to forget. Dad spends a lot of time making tea in the kitchen when they is all together because it all does get very quite noisy and when he says somefing cheeky, they all do say 'shut up!' at the same time.

Anyway, as it is Mother's Day I did fink I would let you know My Forts on Mums:

Mums do almost everyfing. Not HEVERY quite fing but if it is boring or smelly or has to be done again and again and they don't get paid for it, then they do it. This is quite useful for everyboddedy else but not much actual fun for the mums. My Mum generally has to pick up poo in the garden unless she can remember to actual pretend she has a bad back and then Dad moans about the mess and wonders how long before Mum's back is betterer again and can he get away without actual doing it.

Mums are the only peoples who do know wot everyboddedy else in the famberly is doing. Mums do write everyfing down in a diary and very actual yell if people do not look at it or tell anyone wot their plans are. When the fuge ginger boyman is out with his friends and forgets to tell Mum and then gets stranded at the pub because Dad is working and didn't say he was going to be late and the previously ginger one is sulking because she didn't know everyone was going to the pub and she's been left out, Mum has to sort it all out and make sure everyboddedy is still speaking to actual each other.

Mums are the only peoples who know where the freezer is. And that they has to get stuff out of it so you do not actual starve. If Mum is out, Dad does get very quite clear instructions about wot I has to have and when. And then he does get phone calls to make actual sure he has not forgotted to do this because he is too busy clicking Uff.

Mums do all the remembering for actual everyone. Mum reminds the fuge ginger boyman to take his phone with him and reminds the previously ginger one that the world is not going to stop if she do put her phone down for 10 minutes whilst she eats her tea. She do remind Dad when it is a school meeting and reminds him and reminds him and reminds him so that if he was even half finking he might like to forget and stay at home to watch the telly, he is either going to have to come up with a hemergency pretty quickly or have a actual row with Mum. Saying that he can't do somefing because there is a cat sitting on him is likely to actual get him a LOOK with long words and the cat plonked outside the door. That excuse only hever worked once and that was because Mum had been drinking wine. But Dad do try it still very sometimes now. He has even been known to hunt for a cat to put on his lap before he sits down so he can actual get out of doing somefing... anyfink. He do not be knowing wot it is he might be asked to actual do but he finks having a cat on his lap will get him out of it, wotever it is. I do actual fink using cats like this is probabbly quite wrong but it is very actual funny watching Dad trying to hang onto a cat when Mum rattles the food bag.

Mums do caring and loving a very actual lot. Sometimes this do come out as nagging and moaning. Sometimes Mums can seem boring but they got that way being a Mum.

Mums are the only people who can find fings. This is mainly because they is the only person who ever puts fings away. Dad doesn't lose fings because he piles everyfing he owns up in front of Uff so the cats don't sit in front of the screen. Dad says Mum is a hippycrit because she can never find her car keys. Or shut larder doors. Or turn lights out. That's wot Dad says anyway. I do fink he is taking a fuge ignormous risk saying fings like this when Mum is holding somefing sharp or hot but he is brave like that.

Mums do sometimes have to drink wine to actual survive.

I are very pleased with my Mum. She do be shaping up quite very actual well. She do let me sleep on the bed with her when she has a nap during the day and she do remember about my dinners. She hardly ever leaves me on my own and now she has stopped trying to poke fings in my ears, I do fink she is going to be very alright.

APRIL

1 April 2014

Today is the day we do sing Happy Birthday to Gipsy. Gipsy is the oldest cat here and she is 9 years old. She is the most sensible cat who lives here which isn't that much of a very actual compliment. She does keeping 'herself-to-herself' very well unlike the others which are mad. Seriously. The only time Gipsy doesn't keep 'herself-to-herself' is when anyboddedy does invade her space. Those of us with actual brains know that her space is about 15 miles wide. You is actual fine with Gipsy cos you know where you stand; as far away as possible.

It's the weird ones like Mouse you have to watch. One moment she's as nice as anyfink, the next fing you know you are wondering if your eyeballs will actual ever work again.

Mouse's latest trick is to bash you as you walk past. She isn't fussy who she bashes; hoomans are getting bashed too. She has moved from the DVD player and has taken up residence on the telephone table so every so often I hear 'Variations on the Feem of Ow' coming from the hall. The amount of 'Ow' and the additional 'you hateful cat, for blinking hecks SAKE,' (or ruderer words to be quite actual honest) seems to vary according to the amount of clothes people are wearing and the number of times they has been gotted so far that day. Currently, the previously ginger one is coming off worst because she wears the least amount of clothes although Mum is the most hoffended because she can't work out wot she has done to deserve being bashed by a psychotic cat every time she goes to make a cup of tea.

Most of us are wondering why we ever moaned about her living on top of the DVD player. She was only inconvenient there; now she's blinking actual lethal.

2 April 2014

Because I are a luffly boykin, I do get very good food here. That means I are fed a raw diet wot does include raw meaty bones. Yesterday, Mum did give me neck of venison which is one of my very actual favourites. I do like it because it takes ages to eat and I end up with a bit like a tennis ball that I can carry around and have a nibble on and a play with. Sometimes, if Mum is not actual paying attention, I do like to take it into the garden and bury it. But Mum was paying attention yesterday and that didn't happen.

Dad was not paying attention so I tooked it upstairs to have a good old bitey licky session with it on Mum and Dad's bed. When Mum wented upstairs there was a very quite big mucky, fatty wet circle on the bed where I had had a very quite fabumazing time.

Because the washing machine here is currently broken and in bits, Mum couldn't wash the duvet. But it was all very quite ok because it was on Dad's side of the bed and Mum did not tell him. She still hasn't told him...

3 April 2014

Yesterday, I did host my very own first party. How exciting is THAT! Everyboddedy else finks it wasn't a party but I do! Mum says it wasn't a party cos there weren't any hinvitations. Dad says it wasn't a party cos he hates them and he would have banned it. The fuge ginger boyman says it wasn't a party cos there was no vodka and the previously ginger one says it wasn't a party cos she is too busy doing her textiles coursework and could everyone shut up. The fuge ginger boyman says she shouldn't be stressing about these exams; they're only Easy Peasys and 'Worzel could pass them.' Mum did actual get hinvolved and very cross at this point saying that they 'Aren't Easy Peasys, they are GeeSeeEsEees and could he Please. Shut. Up. NOW.' There were some other words mentioned but they is not for plite-comp-knee... No-one, Mum says, should have both children doing exams in the same year. No-one, Dad says, should have children, full stop, given the number of harguments round here currently. But then he did get a Look. From. Mum and bogged off down the boatyard.

Mum also said I shouldn't babble on with selfish talk about my very not party when Gipsy didn't have one for her birthday and would have left home FOR GOOD if she even fort anyone would do somefing so utterly irresponsible in her house. Gipsy does know long words and everyfing cos she is 9.

But I do fink 4 dogs and 3 hoomans on a walk is a party. I was a very plite boykin and did introduce Pip and Merlin to Faye. Everyone found plenty to talk about, especially Pip but then she always does. Merlin did like Faye very much and there was flirting going on. I fort I was very quite special to Faye but it seems she does like Merlin too.

We all did have a super time and I was very proud of myself for sharing my water bowl and showing everyone the best places to sniff and do cocking their leg. Faye did like my muddy puddles very much and Pip was very good at not showing Faye how to bog off or find a nagenda.

I do fink my first party was a great success and Mum says she is very pleased with how my being-good-in-compnee is actual going.

4 April 2014

Today I are feeling like I is the bees knees. I are growing up to be a real dog. I eated my liver. And it was raw, not flash fried like wot baby dogs do get. Lots of raw fed dogs do not be liking to eat liver but I has to have it because it has somefing himportant in it wot is not in other food. It is actual weird stuff though. It is all slimy and wobbly like a jelly wot has goned off. I would find it much actual easier to eat if it could just stay in the same place instead of slithering about everywhere. Sometimes, I do bury it in my bed for a bit. Then it gets dust and hairs stucked all over it. The previously ginger one says this is beyond revolting but at least it gives it a bit of grip so I can get hold of the very actual blinking fing.

6 April 2014

So, the last 48 hours have been very actual different to each other. Yesterday everyone here except Mum had to go to the Dentist. Mum hates going to the dentist, even though the dentist man is very good looking but it is no compensation happarently. Whilst everyone else was having their mouths looked into and tutted over, Mum did take me to the beach where I met a nice doggy friend. He was very quite fun but also shocked at how fast I could go! As far as I are actual concerned, this is how days should go.

Today, though, has been not very nice a-very-tall. Yesterday, Dad did finally fix the 'flipping washing machine before we have nothing to wear except a tuxedo and a wetsuit.' It has been broken for over a week and Mum was starting to get a bit fed up. So, now that it is fixed at-blinking-last, all we has done today is washing, washing, washing. It has been too very busy with piles of stuff everywhere and there is no actual sign of a walk or anyfink.

I fink this is very not fair as I do not make washing for Mum. I have 2 coats. One of these I wear in January only if I absolutely have to cos I look like a plonker in it. The other one I do wear all the time - it being very attached to me. I do my own washing of it in the sea and in muddy puddles and streams. If these are not available I do use my own very tongue. ONCE, I did have to go in the bath but that was because I did find a peaty boggy oily puddle wot Mum didn't very want on the sofa. I have only hever pee'd on Mum and Dad's bed once and also did recently take my dinner up to her bed but that's not a lot of washering!

So... I DO NOT HUNDERSTAND WHY I ARE NOT GOING FOR A WALK COS OF WASHING. IT IS NOT BEING MY ACTUAL QUITE VERY FAULT.

<u>7 April 2014</u>

Everyboddedy is forgived forever about the washing and the boring day and the not going for a walk. I has just been told some fabumazing news. I will shortly be having a friend to stay. Mum and Dad will be doing doggy fostering again now I are settled in.

It is going to be my very quite himportant job to teach my new foster sister to be gentle and polite. This is going to be extra himportant because happarently she is quite FUGE even though she is still a puppy. We has seen a picture of her and she does not look like a Sighthound a-very-tall. She is black and squidgy and doesn't really have any pointy bits. Dad says that's because 'some muppet' decided to cross a Wolfhound with a Bull-Mastiff, which was a 'really spectacular idea in a flat in Birmingham' but at least she is coming into rescue rather than being dumped or getting so bored she eats someboddedy.

Everyboddedy in the famberly is now finking about wot to call the new foster doggy. Dad do always choose the names of his ex-girlfriends or people who he does fancy off the telly. He finks Mum doesn't know this but she says she isn't stoopid. Mum always chooses posh names cos according to the fuge ginger boyman, she is a snob. Mum says she isn't calling some chavvy name endlessly down on the beach in Southwold because she'd never live it down. The previously ginger one comes up with names that are oppymistic, like Destiny or Fortune which can sometimes be quite very overwhelming for a half-starved Lurcher with mange. The fuge ginger boyman can never decide until he sees wot the doggy does look like and takes flipping ages to choose. Mum says if she waited for the fuge ginger boyman to make up his mind, the dog would be neutered, toilet trained and re-homed before he made up his mind.

I do not know wot they will actual decide but I do know it won't be called Maisie, Lily, Milly or Ellie because Mum says there are 17 actual billion dogs looking for a forever home and they is all called those names. It doesn't really matter wot the doggy is called when it is in foster so long as people can very remember it. Finding a memorababble name is hessential so peoples do apply to the right rescue for the correct actual very dog. You'll be very actual quite amazed how many peoples do get completely muddled up and apply for the quite wrong Maisie, Lily, Milly or Ellie from the wrong actual rescue.

9 April 2014

My new foster sister has only been and gone and HARRIVED. She is very chunky and has lots of energy. She does like all my toys and we have already had a game of tuggy toy and bitey-facey. She is almost as tall as me and she is only 4 months old. I have got very hexcited and I are now panting a lot. Mum says she will have to separate us or I will end up having an art attack or somefing cos the new doggy doesn't have an off button and just goes on and on and on... She does not know about doing weesandpoos in the garden but then most foster dogs very quite don't, so everyboddedy is quite actual used to that.

The fuge ginger boyman started to say she do look like a brick somefing but then he did realise Mum was in the room and shutted up. He finks we should call her Fluffy after the dog in the Harry Potter film but the previously ginger one got all sarcastic about how that's 'hardly going to help get her a new home, idiot...' Dad is currently calling her Geroff-My-Head because she do seem to have NO IDEA about wot hoomans are for apart from walking on.

But Mum has said that she would like to call her Pandora (Pandy for short) because a clever lady who did write a book about Adrian Mole crossed over to the rainbow bridge today and one of her bestest characters was called this name. Mum says this is in memory of her. Her name was Sue Townsend. Everyboddedy has agreed it is a fabumazing name. Dad is now calling her Geroff-My-Head-Pandora.

<u>10 April 2014</u>

Dear Pandora

There are not many rules here but this is one I fink is very quite important.

When I are sleeping and a tired boykin please do be leaving me alone. And please do not be doing jumping in my bed to pinch my toys when I are asleep neither. You cannot be doing it quietly and gently cos you is a) 4 months old and b) built like a milk float. And you have feet the size of a tea plate.

If you do remember this very quite himportant rule in future I will not be telling you off with knobs on again,

Love from Worzel.

<u>12 April 2014</u>

Pandy likes to sleep behind the front door. Most dogs, when realising someone is actual trying to open a door would very get up and move out of the way. Not Pandy. She do just carry on lying there so you has to heave on the door to open it with the weight of a fridge leaning against it. Still she does not actual move and Mum says she do weigh a flipping ton. When you do close the door, she does slide back into her favourite position as if nuffink has happened. If you do attempt to persuade her to actual move away from the door, she do just look at you like those protesters wot lie in the middle of the road and go all floppy. That spot in the sun is Pandora's and she will not be moved. There is not a nasty fort in her mind. She doesn't need to have nasty forts, she just opts out and then it's like persuading a rock to talk.

At first we did wonder if Pandy was a bit, well fick, but it turns out she actual isn't; she just hasn't been shown very nuffink. Over the past few days, Mum has been showing Pandora wot hoomans are for. Like playing and making fings hinteresting or providing treats. Because Pandora hasn't had loads of bad hexperiences from hoomans she's getting the idea really blinking quick which is great for her but very actual bad news for me. She is a right show-off. She has learned to do sit already. And she does it all the time, really quickly. It's ok for actual very her. SHE is all squishy and bendy AND she doesn't have gentleman bits.

Mum is teaching Pandy 'It's ok' next because Pandy has Mastiff in her which means she has a really strong instinct to do guarding and barking. Dad says if you can imagine wot Barry White would sound like if he did do a doggy bark, that is wot Pandy sounds like when she does 'who-are-you-why-are-you-coming-in-my-gate' barking. Mum finks that for the benefit of all visitors and the entire home delivery industry, Pandy knowing 'It's ok' so she do relax and come back to Mum is probabbly a good idea. She don't do anyfink when she sees new peoples, she just does barking and standing looking ignormous and hintimidating which is enough to give anyone an art attack. Or pee their pants. The fuge ginger boyman says it's like an unexpected meeting with a 7 foot American Football player in a dark alley; they might have a degree in Fine Arts but you is probabbly not gonna wait around to find out.

'It's ok' is going really well. Mum's been practicing with people who hunderstand dogs but today she decidered to try it out on the man who came to read the meter. Mum said 'It's ok' and Pandy came and stooded all nicely behind Mum being waggy-tailed and relaxed. Fing is, Pandy decidering she is pleased to see you is almost as much of a hexperience as her being a Mastiff guarding dog. Pandy had to go into her crate so she didn't squash the man and sign his keypad in jubilation.

13 April 2014

Me and Pandora did just do waking Dad up. Dad isn't himpressed. He says he doesn't want bitey-facey near his arm-warmy on his beddy-weddy. He did actual use those words. And then he said off. We did do off.

15 April 2014

Mum is getting quite worried about some cats that do live opposite here. The person who should be looking after them seems to have stopped living in our village and only comes back here once a week. Happarently, the woman is going to live somewhere else forever soon and is moving all her stuff very actual slowly.

The fing is, the woman's cats do keep coming into our house through our cat-flap. The situation is very quite driving Mum bonkers because Frank and me has formed the Home Guard Ginger Militia. Between us, we is on duty every day and all night.

Frank is in charge because it was all his very idea in the first place. If he hadn't made a screaming fuss about the other cats coming in, I don't fink I woulda actual noticed. So he is General Frank, leader of the Ginger Militia and I are his right hand dog. None of the other cats can be bothered to join in. They are too busy attacking peoples in the hallway or himagining the world is going to end or being Gipsy.

During the day I is in charge because Frank is... to be honest, I don't know where or wot Frank does during the day but he isn't available. He just goes off somewhere and leaves me in charge to repel the hinvaders. Even though

Pandy isn't ginger, we have letted her join the Home Guard. To be actual honest she is rubbish at it and doesn't know wot she is supposed to be doing; she just likes all the running and woofing and sliding along the wooden floor. Usually Pandy gets there first. She do fink this is because she is super fast but it isn't actual true. Fact is, I do let her go first, so that she hits the kitchen cupboard at the end of the slippery floor and then I slide into a nice squashy Pandy, rather than a hard wooden cupboard with a nasty knob on. Mum says I are a very bad influence and that I are teaching Pandy to chase cats. I are not chasing cats; I never chase the cats wot live here, HEVER. I are defending them and their food bowls and I do fink I deserve a medal.

At night, when me and Pandy is all tucked up in our crates, Frank is on duty. You won't catch him napping. If there's a cat hinvader at 2am, Frank will have a screaming hissing fit and mega yowl-howl-banshee-ninja-freak out at the cat until it do decide to leave.

Mum says she wishes it would all stop. Noboddedy has had a decent night's sleep for a week now, Pandy is going to do herself a hinjury sliding into the cupboard and start to fink chasing cats is ok. Mabel is now terrified of coming in through the cat-flap in case she gets mistaken for an hinvader and ambushed by the Ginger Militia so she's being weirder than ever. Her solution isn't to avoid coming in, she's now avoiding going out and has taken up residence in the loft. When Mum wented up there the other day she founded hevidence of Mabel's new living arrangements and wasn't impressed.

Mum says she's going to lock the cat-flap at night if she can work out where to put a litter tray that me and Pandy can't get to.

<u>17 April 2014</u>

Today, I wented on a social visit to Hotel de Stoven Hall to see Sally-the-Vet and to get Pandy checked out and so she could have her jabs. I wented along to show Pandora that it is a cool place to be. I did greet Sally-the-Vet in a very-pleased-to-see-you-again way which did make Mum breathe a sigh of relief.

The best news is that I are fishally a skinny ribs so I are back on 3 meals a day until I do weigh 25kg. Pandy is also on 3 meals a day because she is only 4 months old and a baby. I was going to say little baby but there is nuffink little about Pandy. She may look cute and cuddly when peoples see photos of her but photos can be deceiving. It's all about scale you see. Pandy looks like a cute ickle Labrador puppy in pictures but she is really the size of Fridge. So we are now calling her Pandy the Fridge. She don't actual care. She is the happiest wrecking ball fridge in the whole wide world!

18 April 2014

I have been showing Pandora my gardening skills. She has been helping lots. I fink I are very quite good at gardening and I are especially exerlent at showing other dogs how to do gardening.

Mum is trying to be quite very positive and that she probabbly wanted to renovate that actual flower bed this year anyway. She has decided to leave well alone until Pandora is dopped SO LONG as we don't help anywhere else.

In other news, since Mum locked the cat-flap at night, all the woman's cats have taken to living in the shed. That means Mum has 'fat chance of ever getting Mabel out of the loft' because the shed is Mabel's usual hiding place. Everyboddedy is getting quite very upset about all the cats now because they are lonely and wandering about looking for new places to live and upsetting all the other cats wot do live round here.

Mum has sended the woman a message about it all because she isn't sure if she knows how unhappy her cats are. Or how pee'd off all the neighbours are getting.

19th April 2014

Today is Easter Saturday so everyboddedy is harguing about Easter Eggs. Mum has gotted everyboddedy an Easter egg except for me which is very ok because I don't actual fancy being sick. Mum says it's about time the previously ginger one and the fuge ginger boyman bought her an Easter egg especially as they both get pocket money. If they don't, then Mum is going to eat the eggs she bought for them. She doesn't care if they say she is being a 'cruel 'busive mummy' and will give them the number for Childline if they like. The fuge ginger boyman is sulking.

20 April 2014

The fuge ginger boyman is not happy. At all. Not only did Mum eat his Easter egg, Pandora has eated his headphones. I hope it was Pandora. Sometimes I do chew fings that I do not realise are actual himportant. Sometimes I do not even know I have dunned chewing until I stand up and there is a pile of plastic very underneath me.

I do fink it must have been Pandora; Mum says it isn't quite possible for one dog to have eated several pairs of shoes, a kindle HAND a pair of expensive headphones without being in the serious dog house. I are not in the serious dog house, so it must have been Pandora. Simple.

21 April 2014

The woman with the lonely cats did get Mum's message and today she did ask to go into the shed to collect then all up. Mum is very actual relieved and did decide not to say anyfink rude about leaving 5 cats alone for days on end and how that wasn't very actual kind or fair on anyboddedy. The woman do seem to like her cats but she is just a bit, well... dopey, Mum finks. Dad and the fuge ginger boyman did come up with some other names but they got tolded to keep the peace and stuff like that. The most himportant fing, Mum says, is that the cats have now gone to their new home, Frank and me can disband the Ginger Militia home guard, everyboddedy can get some sleep and Mabel can stop living in the loft.

<u>22 April 2014</u>

Today I did introduce Pandora to some of my favourite friends, Pip and Merlin. We had a good time and I was very quite good and didn't take Pandora on a guided tour of Suffolk so Mum was very relieved. Pandora does do 'Come' very quite well. And wait. And all that actual hobedience stuff. You can really very quite go off some dogs...

Pip explained the rules of the game to Pandora very well. The rules are these:

1. Pip is in charge.
2. To be actual very quite honest, there is only one rule.

<u>23 April 2014</u>

Pandora is ready for her new famberly now. She is very wonderful and deserves a very quite luffly home, with a big garden and strong walls. Mum says it's a good job she is all ready because she doesn't fink our house will survive if Pandy and I are together for too much longer. Today we has busted the banisters and the handrail fing with the bars going down is all wobbly and going to actual fall apart.

I fink I should tell anyboddedy who wants to dop Pandy that she do snore. And like a train. I has never HEVER heard a noise like it. Mum says once she is a bit less squishy she'll snore less so she isn't going to mention that when she does describe her for potential owners but I forted you should know.

Mum reckons Pandy will get a fabumazing new home because apart from the snoring and the wall breaking and the fridge doing, she is luffly. She is fabumazing with the cats and does do sit really well. I did stop listening at this actual point.

24 April 2014

It is very quite NOT funny when me and Pandora are letted out into the garden at night. I are a good boy and go out nicely. Pandora has to be told and told and TOLD and then plonked outside.

THEN, she does go round to the side of the house, be letting herself into the kitchen by opening the back door, then through the hole in the kitchen door cos she is super squashy and then back to her bed. Mum would like to be cross about this but because Pandy is so pleased with herself it is difficult not to smile.

Watching Pandy squidge through the cat-flap is hunbelievababble I do have to actual say. I has no hidea how she does it because she is ignormous. She is growing so blinking fast, Dad says, he is beginning to fear the door might go the same way as the banisters. He is waiting for her to arrive at her bed wearing the kitchen door as a fashion statement.

MeanWHILE... I have to do barking yips and yells to let everyone know that I have been forgotted about and am stucked in the kitchen because I are not super squishy and I can't get through the cat-flap. And then they all do laughing at me.

26 April 2014

Yesterday Pandora had to have a bath. Cos she was smelly. Now she is all shiny and not smelly. Dad did ask if I would like a bath. I did very quite actual decline his kind offer. In fact, I have started to avoid going in the bathroom in case anyone else finks I might like one. I've got puddles and I've got me tongue. I don't need no bathing or helping with cleaning, even if I do come home looking like I've been playing in a gunk tank and smelling like a cesspit. I are off baths and that is very actual that.

27 April 2014

That sit fing is back again and it's all Pandy's very actual fault. Pandy does sit straight away. All the time. Even when she isn't asked. Like when she wants somefing and finks she can be cute. I hate sitting. A Sighthound hasn't got the bum for sitting. I very quite actual wish that there was no such fing as flipping sitting.

I can do stand. I can do lying down. I can do lying down with all my legs pointed in actual different directions HAND smile at the same time. But I is not sitting quickly or regularly and especially not if Pandora is doing it at the same time.

29 April 2014

The previously ginger one has not been actual well for a week now and everyboddedy is getting more and more worried. I are trying to be helpful by staying out of her way and out of her bedroom. On top of not being well, she is also trying very actual hard to do her school work because of her Easy Peasy GeeSeeEsEees and she do have to take squillions of hexams. It's harder than Hay Levels, she says, because she has to do everyfing, not just the subjects she likes. The fuge ginger boyman did do opening his actual mouth to hargue but then he did stop and not say anyfink. I fink he do realise the previously ginger one is really quite struggling with everyfing at the moment.

Fings got all confuddling tonight because some peoples came to visit. I was actual asleep and then these fuge green men did arrive with loads and loads of big bags. I wanted to have a look at them and help but Mum said no a lot and then did hignoring me. Both me and Pandy got putted in our crates and tolded to go back to sleep. We got given kongs and the door shut on us, so I don't know wot was actual going on upstairs. Mum was worrying that Pandy would start barking, terrify the green men and wake the neighbourhood but Dad pointed out that there was a 'stonking great ambulance with flashing lights outside and they were probably already awake.'

Dad made cuppatea for everyboddedy upstairs and

then came and clicked on Uff in the office whilst the men were upstairs with the previously ginger one and Mum. He said there wasn't enough room for him up there and he didn't know wot to say or do anyway.

30 April 2014

The green men took the previously ginger one to Opital and Mum has been with her all day. Dad has taken the day off work to look after me and Pandy. We has mostly donned sleeping on the bed with him because everyboddedy was up all night with the green men. When Mum came home she was very actual quite knackered. The previously ginger one will be coming home tomorrow which I is glad about because fings have felted strange without her.

MAY

1 May 2014

Last night I did wake everyone up at 4am. Mum fort it was Pandora being naughty in her crate but it was me. I was very quite cross that Pandora had found somefing hinteresting in her crate and I did not have anyfink quite so actual hinteresting. So I did do barking at her.

Mum was not at all happy. When she had worked out wot all the commotion was and wented back to bed, she forgotted to shut my crate HAND she did leave the stair-gate open. So I did go upstairs and spend the rest of the night on her bed.

From my very quite actual point of view, this was all exerlent. Mum is worried that she has setted herself up for trouble.

2 May 2014

Today we wented visiting. We wented to see Maisie, a Cavalier King Charles Spaniel and Granny Mary, who is Mum's granny. When we wented to see them a couple of weeks ago, Mum told Granny Mary that Maisie was too fat. I fink this was actual rude but it is also very quite true. When we weighed her she was FUGE. Maisie was not amused at being weighed especially when Mum found out she is about 10lbs overweight. It seems that Maisie has been sharing all Granny Mary's snacks and dinners and cakes and biscuits and she was the same shape as a very ball! So, Mum told Granny Mary to put Maisie on a diet. No more snacks for Maisie.

We weighed Maisie today and she has lost about 3lbs. We fink. We're not completely sure because Mum can't remember wot she was wearing or if she tooked her shoes off which is pretty actual daft but she has had a very actual lot on her mind recently. Hunfortunately, Maisie remembered all about being weighed and struggled like a furious frog. All in all, it wasn't wot you'd called scientific. How-very-ever, Maisie is definitely not the same shape as a ball anymore and there is the beginnings of a waist. I do not know wot a waist is but happarently I have one and now so does Maisie.

Maisie tolerates me. She does not like to play much but quite likes watching me being a hidiot. I was a friendly boy and not too very bouncy so Maisie will like me more and more, Mum says. Granny Mary finks I are a luffly boykin and I fink she is super too. She loves it when I wiggle up to her and she laughs when I stretch all across the floor.

<u>5 May 2014</u>

****FANFARE AND DRUM ROLL****

Today on my very actual walk I did do it! I did cock my leg when I didded a wee. I was out for a manly walk with my Dad and it happened. Mum is not pleased because she has been waiting for me to do this for a while now and she MISSED it and tolded Dad off for not taking a photograph. Dad reckons the kids got away lightly being borned before there were digital cameras.

I did have to spend a very quite actual long time on my lead because I was very naughty about coming back. Dad says I have the recall of a golf ball. But you know that fing about dogs chasing sheep? Well, I did not do that. When we were walking on our lead through the sheep field though, THEY did chase US. It was quite very confuddling and scary.

The reason I have been doing manly walks with Dad is that there has been some bad news here. The previously ginger one has had to go to another Opital. The Opital is all the way down in Southampton which means I won't get to be seeing her for an actual whole month. Mum and Dad are very quite hupsetted about this.

The fuge ginger boyman has gone to stay with Granny Annie for the time being so that he does get his dinners and yelled at about going to sleep because of his hexams. Mum says if she leaves him with Dad then they will stay up all night playing on Uff and the fuge ginger boyman will not pass his Hay Levels and will have to become a butcher not a scientist. Happarently, this is a bad fing. I fink it could have some actual benefits but it seems I don't get a vote.

Mum is spending half her time in Southampton and half her time in Suffolk but most of the time fighting her way round the M25 and crying. She is very actual worried about everyfing. Dad keeps saying the previously ginger one is in the right place and she will get betterer but then he goes into the kitchen and does manly worrying on his own.

6 May 2014

I have just been invited to submit a photo of me, Mr. Worzel Wooface for a calendar for Hounds First Sighthound Rescue. I have submitted lots of photos to be in with a good chance. I are actual very quite hopeful because I have stayed with 3 of the 4 judges at some point in my life and they have all said I is a booful boykin. I have it in writings as well.

9 May 2014

When Mum came home from the Opital she did notice somefing that has completely passed Dad by and she is absolutely furious, she says. When the dopey woman came to collect her cats wot were living in our shed, she didn't bother to tell Mum she hadn't caught them all. She has actual left one behind. She is no longer 'the dopey woman.' She is now 'the stupid, selfish woman.' Yesterday, Mum caught a glimpse of the cat wot got lefted behind, hiding behind the dinghy in the shed. As if that wasn't bad enough, the cat is a girl cat and quite actual triangle shaped which means it's going to have babies very actual soon, she finks.

11 May 2014

It's taken Mum two days to catch the stray cat. Finally today, she managed to trap her in the shed but then she didn't do communercating actual proper like. She wented into the house to get the cat basket and whilst she was doing this Dad let the stray cat escape. Things gotted quite loud and words like stoopid, unfinking and mind-reader started flying about. It was one of those conversations that is never going to end unless someboddedy did acting like a grown up. 'You let her out...You didn't say what you were doing... It should have been obvious... Why should it have been obvious?' I wented and hid in my crate because it all got very quite noisy but then, all the harguing did suddenly stop when Dad caughted sight of the cat sneaking back into the shed. Mum and Dad did epic teamwork and managed to get her trapped and crated and fed and blanketed and all calmed down from being caught; and then they forgived each other for being plonkers. They is actual very quite all stressed about the previously ginger one and missing her and worrying about her. It does make hoomans act very quite different when they is being stressed to the eyeballs.

There has been no discussion about wot they plan to do with the cat now it has been caughted. Dad says he knows betterer than to do or say anyfink other than wot he is actual told. Mum is so upsetted bout the previously ginger one that anyfink being a distraction is a good fing.

Mum can't get to Southampton as often as she would like because it costs too much monies and the previously ginger one is miserable and missing Mum and Dad. It's all a total nightmare according to Dad and if that means he has to help look after a stray cat for a few weeks then that's wot is going to have to happen. That's when Mum mentioned the triangle-shape and the kittens and...

Sometimes, my Dad is an actual saint you know. On the phone to the previously ginger one, he did even mention the pregnant stray cat, heven though he knew wot she would say. She's got somefing to look forward to now, Mum says. Dad says, he's got weeks of emptying litter trays and managing 2 nutty Lurchers to look forward to, plus the actual very fact that We. Will. Be. Keeping. One. He is resigned to the fact he says. Mum smiled tonight.

13 May 2014

There is very actual hexcitement here today because a famberly are hinterested in dopping Pandy. Mum has readed their bits of paper and they sound hideel. They has already got 2 fuge dogs already that Pandy won't squash and they seem a bit nutty about their pets which Mum does fink is generally a good fing and so do I. Anyone who takes on Pandy is going to need to be a bit nutty. And have strong walls of their house. Mum and the lady of the famberly did chatting on the phone tonight and Mum asked her lots and lots of very questions about her famberly and her other dogs and her actual 'lifestyle.' Mum asked all very quite personal questions which made Dad cringe and whisper 'you can't ask her THAT' but Mum says she doesn't care. If Pandy is going to live with these peoples then Mum will find out everyfing she can about them, even if the lady finks Mum is nosey. Or rude. Or mad.

Mum has arranged for the lady to come and visit on Saturday. The man in the famberly won't be coming on the visit with the lady (which is a bit actual worrying for Mum because she do like to meet everyboddedy in the famberly) but she will be bringing her growed up daughter instead.

The worst fing, Mum says, is that if they do like Pandy, they would actual like to take her that day because they do live a very long way away. This is giving Mum wobbles because she do usually like people to go away and fink about fings for a few days before making a final actual decision. If you ask me, anyone who goes away and finks about Pandy living in their house will very quite need ferapy.

15 May 2014

The stray cat is getting ignormous at the triangle end but is still skinny everywhere else. She has been living in Mum and Dad's bedroom for the past week or so and is eating for Ingerland. She was doing quite actual well and was being allowed to wander about the bedroom but today she did start looking for places to hide and make nests. Her first choice of places to hide was rubbish. We all did find her. Mum says she's going to need socks over the next 2 months so her underwear drawer is actual out. Then the stray did decide that a hard shelf five feet off the floor would be an exerlent place to have her babies which would be ok if she was having seagulls but she isn't. Mum finks a nest somewhere nearer the ground might be actual safer. So the stray cat is going into a crate and going to live in the previously ginger one's bedroom to have her kittens where it is quiet. Mum is sad about this. The room shouldn't be actual empty.

The stray hasn't been named as very such. She has just growed the name Stray which doesn't usually happen here. The previously ginger one would never, HEVER have allowed this. She would have actual insistered that Stray was given a proper name. Everyboddedy has got too much actual on their minds at the moment and seems to have forgotted about naming the stray.

No-one is allowed to get excited about cute-ickle-kittens because according to Dad it could all go horribly wrong and there be no kittens at the end. The stray is too young to be having actual babies and half starved as well so noboddedy is allowed to be getting their hopes up.

The fuge ginger boyman says he is 'working his bum off' at Grannie Annie's for his Hay Levels. And getting fat. He's getting a cooked breakfast every day so he has actual decided to stay at Grannie Annie's until after his hexams are over. Mum says she can't compete with a cooked breakfast every morning and anyway, Grannie Annie has the world's worst broadband connection, so he can't play confuser games which is probabbly all a good fing. Mum is ever so very actual proud of him for being so serious and growed up about his hexams and she's glad it's one less fing she has to worry about.

18 May 2014

It's very quiet here today because my foster sister has gone to her Probabbly-Almost-Definitely Forever Home. Mum says that nuffink is for very definite in the first few days but she is very actual, very quite pleased with Pandy's new famberly, Dawn, Zoe and Mike.

When the lady, Dawn, and her daughter Zoe comed into the house, Mum and Dawn did chit-chat for a few minutes so Pandy could check the lady out through the hole in the door to the kitchen. Mum wented to open the door and when she did turn round Dawn was sat on the floor. Mum was quite actual hembarrassed about this because it was covered in muddy foot prints but Dawn didn't seem to care. She sat on the floor and said nuffink. She sat and waited until Pandy did come up and have a sniff. STILL she did do nuffink. Pandy was quite actual insistering that the lady do somefing and so Dawn did put her hand in a place where Pandy could nudge it. All the time this was going on Mum did chatting to Zoe, the lady's daughter and did big, BIG sighs of actual relief. Dawn was far more interested in Pandy than in Mum which is how it should actual be. Mum fort she was very kind and clever. The lady knew very quite well how to get Pandy to relax and to talk to her.

Pandy did do leaning into Dawn, who must be very actual quite strong or used to it because she didn't do toppling over or nuffink. If Pandy leans on me, I do generally find myself hupside down. Pandy forted the lady was fabumazing. I did like her too but that wasn't wot very actual mattered. I checked them out but then I left them to it. Mum came through to see me and Dad. She did do a lot of hissing quickly at Dad that this famberly could be perfick and that she was crossing her fingers that Dawn and Zoe would like Pandy. Dad did have a stroll through to check them out and make a cuppatea because he did want Pandy to be happy about it all as well. The lady and her daughter did stay for an hour sitting on the kitchen floor and after that, the lady did say 'Yes. I do fink Pandy will fit in very well in our home.'

Mum and Dad has dunned lots of fostering in the past but Mum says this is the most actual comfortable she has HEVER felt about handing a doggy over.

I keep forgetting Pandy has goned to her forever home and I has been wandering around looking for her. She definitely has not come back in the night. I are a bit sad about this because I did love our bitey-facey games. On the bright side, I was allowed to sit on the sofa last night to watch the telly AND I don't have to be protected from the stampeding-food-stealing-munch-monster wot is Pandy when I eat my dinner.

Everyboddedy is moping a bit because they do miss Pandy but Mum has started finking about rescuing her garden and Dad is wondering how the hell he is going to fix the banisters.

I are mainly alright and being spoilt lots but I do miss my Pandy a bit. I hope she will be very quite actual happy and that her new home works out brilliantly.

19 May 2014

Mum gotted a message today from Dawn who has dopped Pandy. This is wot it did say:

Well I think you could say that Pandy Pants has made herself at home and quite likes Lincolnshire. At the moment she is fast asleep on the sofa with me and Mr. Blue Dude is asleep on the other side of the sofa, Miss Anamcara and Mr. Sparky are out in the dining room flaked out on the slate tiles snoring after their lunch.

I hope Worzel won't mind too much but Pandora says she missed him on the way here in the car but says she has a smashing new chase me, chase me chum called Blue. But Worzel also needs to know that she says I am not going to be coming back to Suffolk, I love my new mummy and daddy and my new pack mates. I have not quite made friends with the oldest lady dog I have ever seen, she truly is a real granny of a dog and she is a grumpy old bag but I think I will love her as much as I love Blue Dude and Sparky too but Blue Dude is my bestest pal next to you Worzel, he even shares his snacks with me.

Oh... on the way back in the car yesterday my daughter Zoe said 'Pandy is not right for her, mum' and I had to agree, we have called her Gypsy, she responds to it straight away and it really suits her.

So, I fink that is very actual quite that, and Pandy has been dopped and has her forever actual home. I cannot actual believe she wanted to be called Gypsy though. Who would want to be named after the most actual scariest cat in the whole wide very world?

20 May 2014

Mum didn't go to bed last night because Stray did do giving birth to her kittens and Mum did hobserving and very Being There in case everyfing wented pear-shaped. It all started at 1am and I was not allowed to join in. I did get to do sleeping with Dad on the bed and also I-don't-care-what-he-does-you-just-make-sure-he-is-quiet-and-doesn't-get-out. I did this very actual exerlently and did not know about the giving birth fing until this morning.

There are five kittens and Mum says they is all alive and

about the same size. Mum says that is good news because there isn't one she has to worry and flap about. Dad says that just means she'll worry and flap about all five of them. There are two tabby ones and 3 black ones. I did walk past the bedroom this morning and my appearance did not cause chaos or ninja-hissy-fits from Stray so I are not going to be banned from upstairs for the next 2 months which I is very quite relieved about.

The fing Mum is worrying about at the moment is that she only counted 4 placentas and there were 5 kittens. There should have been one for each actual kitten. These are the fings that keep the kittens alive inside the mummy cat and they should all have comed out. It's very not ok for it to still be stuck inside her. Happarently cats do eat this placenta fing and that is very ok. If I did eat somefing which came out of me, I would be called disgustering but that's cos only weesandpoos comes out of me.

Mum phoned Sally-the-Vet about the placenta fing. Sally-the-Vet says to watch Stray and if she does start being poorly-sick then she is to bring her straight to see her.

Stray is not feeling poorly-sick at all although Mum says she nearly had a panic attack in the afternoon because Stray did decide to do bogging off which is normal-but-not-helpful. Mum says she did fink that on top of worrying about the previously ginger one in Opital in Southampton and the fuge ginger boyman's Hay Levels, she was also going to have to hand rear 5 kittens. This was all to very much for Mum to worry about so after about 20 minutes she did go and get stray out of the garden and lock her in the crate. It is all very actual tough if Stray doesn't like it. Mum can't be dealing with anyfink else.

This evening Mum was supposed to go to the theatre to see her friend Louise in A Musical. A Musical is when people do manic jumping up and down and dancing and singing, so I is not actual surprised Louise was inned it; Louise's life is a permanent musical but with more mud. Just before she was going to leave, Mum wented to check on the kittens and Stray and she fort she could see and feel somefing hard and kitten shaped inside the mummy cat. Mum did have a big panic and phoned Sally-the-Vet who said Stray and the 5 kittens needed to come to the Hotel de Stoven Hall straightaway.

Sally-the-Vet said there was no more kittens. I fink Sally-the-Vet did feel a bit sorry for Mum missing the theatre because when she got her purse out to pay, Sally-the-Vet did tell Mum to go home and get some sleep and not be worrying about the monies. Mummy was feeling like a bit of a wally for panicking and even more so an hour later, when Stray did the biggest poo you have ever seen come out of a cat.

So far Mum has been called a prat, a wally, a hidiot and a numpty. Mainly by herself.

<u>21 May 2014</u>

The previously ginger one is missing everyboddedy very much and Mum says this can't go on any longer. Southampton is too far away and not having famberly close by can't be helping and is probabbly doing more harm than good. Mum is SO angry there isn't a nearer Opital. The previously ginger one did try to do one of her hexams yesterday in the Opital but she got all muddled up and learned all the wrong fings. The previously ginger one told the person sitting in with her that she wasn't going to do it cos she'd only cock it up. Mum said she must just try to do her best and that it didn't matter at all. The fact that she was trying was as good as passing them as far as she was concerned.

All the kittens are doing actual well and Mum decided to see if she could have a look to see whether they were boys or girls. She finks that both the tabby cats are boys and the black ones are 2 girls and a boy. Mum has letted everyboddedy know about this which I fink is actual quite brave because sexing kittens in blinking actual difficult, especially at a day old. How-very-ever, if she is actual right, then she has got 2 fantastic homes organised for three of the kittens and as We. Will. Be. Keeping. One. then that only means that a new home is needed for Stray and the male black kitten.

Dad cheered right up when he heard all this. He fort we were going to be keeping Stray HAND a kitten. So fings are only half as bad as he forted they was going to be and he is breathing big sighs of relief. To be actual very fair, Dad do luffs the cats. Before he metted Mum he had not had a dog but he had hadded a cat. A cat. One cat. Not four. Or now five. He does very wonder sometimes why everyfing here happens in extra large.

<u>22 May 2014</u>

I have just had a hupset. I was having a super snooze outside my crate wot I do sleep in and wot is my safe place. I did do roll over and somehow managed to roll under the door and then I gotted stuck.

I was very quite actual frightened and when I did try to struggle out in a panic I did get even more stucked. So I did squeal and yell and wriggle.

This was my bestest, safest place where I do hide all the toys and the best bits of blanky (and other more hinteresting fings to be honest - Mum founded a dead mouse in there hagain the other day wot I did pinch off the cats) and NOW I DO NOT LIKE IT AND I ARE NOT GOING IN IT NO MORE!

<u>23 May 2014</u>

Seeing as I won't go in my crate anymore, Mum has putted it away. She says she's been finking about it for a while seeing as I mainly use it for stashing away disgustering fings and seem to be spending most nights sleeping on her and Dad's bed since Pandy went. I've been setted up with a new safe place under a table in the office which is very actual quite secluded but easier for Mum and Vera to de-yuck. I are very pleased with this new arrangement and so is Mum. She says she forgets how much room a crate takes up; when you dismantle them it feels like you has had an hextension.

The previously ginger one has managed to do 2 hexams in Opital which everyboddedy do fink is gobsmacking. Mum is going to Southampton again this weekend and says she is hoping the previously ginger one can come home soon. We is all feeling betterer about this but Dad says there will be no foreign trips on the boat this year because the 'poxy guv'ment can't find an Opital closer to home' and we've spended all our monies on petrol. There will be some trips but nuffink as expensive or long as we did actual very hope for.

24 May 2014

I wonned! I wonned! I are now a calendar boykin. I are Mr. April in the calendar. I do look gorgeous and very yellow because the photo was tooked in a field of oil seed rape. Mum says that's all her Christmas shopping sorted!

27 May 2014

When Mum was at the Opital at the weekend, she was actual shocked that the peoples there said they wanted the previously ginger one to stay there for another 10 weeks. Mum did say No. Loudly. In lots of different ways. With knobs on. Everyboddedy has had a-very-nuff, especially the previously ginger one, who Mum says would never actual forgive her if she lefted her there any longer. So, she is coming home at the beginning of June and it is actual like somebodddedy just opened the curtains here. Everyboddedy is walking about faster, running up the stairs, talking cheerfully and being very actual busy harranging stuff.

I wonder if anyboddedy did mention to the previously ginger one that she has an actual cat and 5 kittens and a smelly litter tray in her room at the moment. It's beginning to smell quite actual fabumazing from my point of view but I do be hunderstanding that eau-de-kittens-and-litter trays isn't everyboddedy's actual very favourite smell.

28 May 2014

Today Mum and Dad are celebrating being together for 10 actual whole years. To be very actual quite honest, that isn't really true; they is wondering where the time wented and how the hell they've managed it. So is Grannie Annie. She did say when she first metted Dad that he was an 'opportunistic philanderer' and that it would last six weeks. You might fink that Dad would be quite actual offended being called an 'opportunistic philanderer' but he is not. He is very, very proud of it and reminds Grannie Annie about it all the time. He says that seeing as he is 51, completely grey and has a dodgy elbow HAND a wonky knee, it's pretty cool. This makes Grannie Annie hopping-mad-cross because he's not supposed to be actual pleased about it. She did very mean it when she said it but now she pretends she said it as a challenge to make sure he didn't bog off. Noboddedy does believe her. Dad likes to remind her a lot that she was wrong. Grannie Annie doesn't do being wrong very well at all.

Mum is very quite pleased because Dad did actual remember this hanniversary. He didn't have a lot of choice to be quite very honest because she's been reminding him for the last month. Mum has too many hanniversaries, Dad finks; the day they gotted married, the day they met, the day they moved in together. He forted if they gotted married that would be the only one he would have to actual remember. It seems not. Mum says if he could actual remember the day they got married and even perhaps her birthday, then maybe she'd not go on about all the others. Me and Dad aren't convinced.

Dad is rubbish at remembering hanniversary stuff and Mum doesn't actual help sometimes. Dad spent an hentire year telling everyboddedy he was 43 when he actual wasn't. Mum did the Maths wrong when he asked her how old he was and so he had to have 2 years being 43 and never gotted to be 42. Now they have remembered this hincident, they've moved on from wondering how they managed to stay together for 10 years and now they is wondering if they actual have. But the fuge ginger boyman has checked the Maths and says it is very true, so Dad has boughted flowers, Mum has made Dad's favouritist dinner and everyboddedy is wondering if they will last another 10 years. Grannie Annie isn't saying a word.

29 May 2014

I did pinch a carrot wot Mum did drop. I don't be doing this very hoften so when I did take the carrot off the floor, I did not actual get told off. In very fact, Mum was frilled to bits with this normal-dog-behaviour and finks there is hope for me yet. Trouble is, I do not know wot to do with it now cos I don't actual want to eat it but it feels like a prize. Happarently, this isn't normal-dog-behaviour and very definitely not normal-Sighthound-dog-behaviour. Most Sighthounds would not be carrying it around; it would have been eated in a flash even if they didn't like it cos they is food-stealing-munch-monsters.

I don't fink I'm much good at this aspect of Sighthounding. Mum says this isn't actual a problem from her point of view; she's met some Sighthound food thieves, she says, and they do defy very belief.

The most himpressive thieves she hever did meet were a pair of quite elderly Italian Greyhounds or Iggies. Mum hinsists Iggies are pure Sighthound but I do fink, from wot she's tolded me, that they have monkey buried somewhere in their jeans cos they can climb anywhere.

The Christmas before I did arrive here, Mum was hinvited to a Sighthound party and got the chance to meet up with one of her foster dogs, Suzy. Suzy, a long tall Lurcher lady, actual had a rubbish life before she was fostered and dopped; so she did do protectering everyfing - her toys, her bed, her food - every actual fing.

To make sure Suzy wasn't wanting to protect the food at the party, lots of fings were put up very high so that she wouldn't be actual worried and do guarding or food-pinching. Suzy did relax and everyboddedy else did very too, finking that if the food was out of long, tall Suzy's reach, then noboddedy else would very quite be able to get at it.

But they did forget about the Iggies. You should never, hever forget about Iggies, hespecially wise and ancient Iggies wot do know every actual trick in the very book and who managed to get up onto the top of a fridge freezer without anyboddedy noticing.

Mum says seeing these 2 tiny Iggies staring down at her from above her head and covered in cake was actual the funniest and weirdest fing she has ever seen.

Like lots of peoples who like Sighthounds, Mum secretly does want an Italian Greyhound but she would only hever dop a dog and they don't come into rescue very actual often. I find this very hard to hunderstand...

30 May 2014

I have decidered that I aren't going to be flea-treated. I are doing hiding in my bed and not coming out. Every time Mum does appearing, I does hiding. I do not want anyfink touching my actual neck. It's my neck and it's my choice. Mum says that's all very well and good but we currently have 10 blinking cats in the house and it's nearly summer and she isn't hosting the world flea convention in her bed.

The fuge ginger boyman did come home this evening and so he and Mum came up with a cunning plan. I did go all waggy-tail-where-you-been-WOW-Grannie-Annie-has-a-lot-of-dogs and while I was hinvestigating this very actual hinteresting fact all over his trousers, he did drop the stuff on me. I do feel betrayed and conned and all other kinds of tricked fings. But then he did take me out with Fizzy for some epic puddle jumping fun so I has forgived him.

The fuge ginger boyman was all actual pleased with himself for getting the flea treatment on me, until Mum pointed out that you're supposed to keep dogs dry for a day after applying the flea treatment. He pointed out that my neck was still actual dry and Mum is hoping that's good enough because there's no way she finks I are falling for that trick again. And she's right.

JUNE

1 June 2014

All the kittens have gotted their eyes open now and they all have two which seem to work. Mum's levels of pessimism are at an all time high, Dad reckons, seeing as she was finking that they might not. The previously ginger one is due to come home at the end of the week and until she is home Dad reckons that Mum is going to be all over the place, so we might as well just do saying 'yes, dear' a lot. The fuge ginger boyman tried saying it tonight. I don't fink he'll be doing it again.

Mum was right about wot sex the kittens be. There is 3 boy ones and 2 girl ones. We is going to be keeping one of the tabby boy ones but the name finking will not start until the previously ginger one comes home.

The two black girls will be going together to live in Chelmsford. The peoples who are having them are about to get married and I fink the kittens are a kind of wedding present to themselves. The man has never had a pet ever before and he is very, very actual excited and reading everyfing he can about having pets and kittens. We does all actual approve of this because having a pet is a big decision wot should be actual taken very seriously.

Dad says I'm growing so much that I are not a big decision anymore; I is a fuge ignormous blinking great lummox wot he can hardly lift and 'whatever happened to the idea of a small dog that will fit on the boat.'

2 June 2014

Mum is starting to seriously panic about the 3 peaks walk fing now. Wot with the kittens and the previously ginger one, she is very behind in her training. Some very nice peoples from a gym in Lowestoft have gived her and Louise free access so that they can pretend to be walking up hills because there aren't any real ones in Suffolk. Mum has been going on this stair-walking machine and can walk to the top of a skyscraper in 15 minutes now. The first time she did it, she said it took 20 minutes and she did nearly pass very out. She hopes she'll have enough actual training done if she keeps going at this rate and is quite actual pleased at how fast she can do the step fing now compared to a week ago.

The biggest problem Mum has now is that her foot has been hurting the last couple of times she has dunned some training. Dad reckons her biggest problem is that she is fat and forty-somefing but he's decided not to tell her that. I do fink this is wise and so he is listening lots to Mum wail about her poorly toe instead. It has been wonky since she was 15 but all the walking recently has reminded her toe to start hurting again. She is trying to find some boots for the walk that will stop her toe bending too actual much but at the same time not give her blisters everywhere else. The best she can come up with is her wellies but noboddedy does fink the horganisers will let her walk in them. Especially as they are 20 years old, used to belong to Grannie Annie and don't have any tread left on the bottom of them.

3 June 2014

Stray has gotted a forever home! When she has finished being a mummy cat, she is going to live in the countryside with lots of fields and a fuge pond. Mum is very pleased about this because she has had a rubbish start to her life and deserves somefing good and special to happen. The lady who is dopping Stray says there is a platform in the middle of the pond and she does very hope that Stray is not going eat the baby ducks wot do sometimes live on there. They is going to try and position the platform so that Stray can't reach them cos eatering the baby ducks would be a very actual bad fing.

I do actual fink that the peoples are worrying about the wrong fings to be very quite honest. There is actual very no chance of Stray eatering the baby ducks. When they do see her coming, the ducks will do the swimming fing that cats are very rubbish at. The very actual fing they should be worrying about is somefing called Motivation. This is when you do get a fabumazing hidea that you can actual hachieve somefing himpossible. And that can get you into very trouble.

Motivation can get you stucked on the wrong side of a ditch cos you were chasing a crow, or locked in the kitchen cos you can't squidge through the whole or... completely actual wedged under the bed trying to get a hinteresting fing wot has gotted kicked hunder there wot you really actual definitely need to have.

So, Stray might have very actual quite lots of motivationing to climb the tree that hangs over the pond and then epic motivationing to leap from the tree in the very direction of the duck pond... but then the motivation will suddenly bog off, just like the ducks who will swim off the moment she does the leaping fing from the tree. Stray will then very actual discover she is in fuge trouble and it wasn't such a very fabumazing idea hafter all.

The only way out of motivation is hoomans. You very often have to actual wait for them to stop laughing or panicking first and that can take a quite long time. Then, you has to put up with them trying to persuade you to unstuck yourself or coming back by yourself. It can take flipping ages for them to work out that you are not very quite stoopid and would have donned that already if you actual could. And then you has to wait for them to dismantle the bed around you. And take all the stuff hunder the bed out and then tut about all the bits of yuck that have been under there for 10 years and then hargue about the book that Dad accused Mum of leaving in a cafe that she didn't because it was Hunder. The. Bed. The. Whole. Time. As you can probabbly tell, I is hexperienced in the disasters of motivation quite very actual badly.

Once you has got unstucked and checked for hinjuries, the himportant fing is to remove yourself from the situation all quick and in a not-bothered-a-very-tall sort of way, so that hoomans don't do discussing it with you. Hoomans do fink that just after they has unstucked you is the bestest time for talking to you about being a hidiot. It is very not. When I has been a plonker, I do not want to talk about it; I want to do pretending it didn't actual happen.

I fink Mum and Dad should be actual happy about this. That way, they can get on with putting their bed back together again and finish the hargument about the book that didn't get lefted in the cafe.

4 June 2014

I did go to work with Dad and did management in the office because I still don't like it if Dad bogs off and leaves me in the yard. Everyfing at work is warmer now and the peoples do sit outside for their cuppatea breaks. That means I do get to see all the dogs wot go walkies down at the harbour. And Dad do get to see all the ladies doing joggering. All the men and dogs do say hello to the joggerers. The dogs do smiley-waggy-tail-luffly-boykins to the joggerers faces and the men do smiling at their bottoms. I aren't very allowed to say anyfink about this to Mum, as she has goned to collect the previously ginger one from Southampton and it probabbly won't go down too actual well.

5 June 2014

The kittens have been moved down into the sitting room. That's so the smell of litter trays can waft around the entire house, Dad says. All of the kittens have dunned staying alive and we have all stopped worrying that Stray would not be able to cope. I do find the kittens hinteresting but I do not consider them edible, which everyboddedy do fink is a fuge actual relief because there is only so many ways that the hanimals here can be kept actual apart.

Stray has taken to leaving the kittens and coming into the hall for a snooze with me each morning and we share the bit of sunshine that comes in at that time of day. Well, to be actual fair, she just comes along and tells me to budge up so she can have some of it, or she just lies down next to me when I are asleep. I don't fink she realises that I is a Sighthound; I are not even sure she do realise I are a dog. She is setting a very good example to her kittens, Mum says.

The other cats do all fink she is a traitor for cuddling up with me. They is all refusing to leave the kitchen because they don't want to walk past the sitting room. I do fink Stray would do hignoring them as much as she hignores me but they is sulking very big time.

7 June 2014

*** HIMPORTANT NEWS ***

The previously ginger one is home! She do look very pale and hinteresting and is very actual tired and doing a lot of sleeping. I have been mainly keeping out of her bedroom and being a good boy which is quite very easy because I are a luffly exerlent boykin. You would have fort that being in Opital would get you a good hexcuse not to do any more hexams but the poor previously ginger one has got another one on Monday wot she is revising for. She seems to want to do it which everyboddedy do fink is very strange and very himpressive at the same time. It's

Maths which she is ok about. I'm not sure if it doesn't bother her because she don't like Maths and so doesn't give a stuff or if she is really exerlent at it and can do it without finking. Dad says we'll find out in August.

The fuge ginger boyman's Hay Levels start on Monday as actual well. He has 'worked hincredibabbly hard for them and Mum is very scared. He has tried so actual his very best and has had to deal with all the stuff with the previously ginger one at the same time so Mum has everyfing crossed that they go well. The fuge ginger boyman looks like he is very actual relaxed about them; he has dunned the Maths and he knows hexactly how many points he needs to get on each hexam to get the grades he needs to go to Universally. I just do hope that he is as good at Maths as the previously ginger one seems to be. Dad says we will find out about that in August as well. I aren't looking forward to August.

8 June 2014

Pip and Merlin have got compnee like they say round here. He is a friendly old chap called Max wot I do like very much. He is everyfing dog-shaped that I are not. He is heavy and lumbery and squishy. I are bony and wiggly and all legs. When we stand next to each other we make each other look very actual quite reedickerless. I do look like I are starving and needing lots of dinners and he do look like a miniature hippypottymiss. If you did see either of us on our very own, you would not fink anyfink was wrong but together we look hawful. Mum tries not to look at us at the same time which was quite easy today because I was being actual very careful supervised closely so she couldn't look too much at Max as well. This is because Ghost did come on our walk as well. Ghost is a German Shepherd Dog wot lives with Claire across the road and he is the first actual dog I have met who a very little bit reactive, which means if I do annoy him, he will get actual proper cross. Pip do get cross sometimes but it is cross like wot a headteacher does; you know they is hannoyed but you know they isn't going to eat you. Ghost can very sometimes get the other cross - the one that is actual flipping scary and Mum was quite very keen I did do behaving proper like.

But I did! I was very exerlent. The first time I met Ghost he did his I-is-scary-with-knobs-on-go-away-you-whipper-snapper so I did going away flipping actual very fast but today I did approach a little bit more actual carefully and although Ghost did deep woofy barking, he did then start to play chase. Once you realise that Ghost is chasing you for actual fun and not because he is going to eat you, it is all very fabumazing. It is a bit like being chased up the stairs by your big sister or somefing. It feels scary and frilling but you know you aren't really going to die if you get catched! It was great to be chased by a dog wot can at least pretend he might be able to keep up with me. Merlin is fabumazing for bitey-facey and Pip is super fast in 3 metres shrieking bursts but usually, I start to run, look behind me and I've gone hundreds of actual metres before they've even take 6 little steps.

Everyfing wented actual quite well on the walk until we founded smelly ditch. And then it got even betterer! The bottom of the ditchy river fing was pure, stinky, sticky black mud. Me and Merlin wented in first. Merlin, being the smallest Lurcher in the whole wide world, kind of skittered over the top so he didn't sink but my legs wented straight down and I ended up looking like I was wearing black stockings. Then Max did decide that seeing as he looks like a hippypottymiss, he would very act like one and came plunging into the smelly ditch. He did do epic sinking and splashing around and gotted completely covered in mud. Mum, Louise and Claire did fink it was super and smashing watching us all having a fabumazing time and didn't really care about the smelly mud.

Until we gotted to the stile. Mum and Louise realised that they was going to regret the ditch fing, big very actual time. Mum did bravely have to lift me over first and that was bearababble because most of my mud was on my feet and legs. But have you hever tried to lift a hippypottymiss over a stile? Max weighs a lot and a lot and then some actual more and it took Mum and Louise every single bit of strength to get the old chap over the stile. He did find this very actual quite undiggernafied and did struggling and objectoring which didn't-blinking-help-Max-you-great-oaf. Most of Max's mud ended up on Mum and Louise and they have decidered that from now on, HONLY dogs which can get over stiles by their own selves are allowed in smelly ditches.

11 June 2014

Today is the hanniversary of when Charlie, my famberly's first doggy died. It is a very fortful day for my famberly but not as sad as many people might actual fink. It's been 3 years since he did die. Mum and Dad remember Charlie with a lot of happiness because they is not upset about how he died.

His last 4 years being alive were quite actual hard work for him. He did have creaky bones which did hurt and did not be able to know when to do weesandpoos. This didn't bother him a-very-tall but was very sometimes a bit hembarrassing for Mum and Dad when they did have plite-comp-knee but Charlie did live here and that was very that. If the plite-comp-knee didn't like it, they could not come again.

Having the foster dogs to boss about did give Charlie lots of hinterests in his old age and kept him going with somefing to moan about and get up and down to see wot was wot. He did heven enjoy going out to play with the foster dogs and did like to try to trot after their toys. But by June 2011, even this was too actual much for him and it gotted to the stage where Charlie was not liking being alive any more.

Peoples do say that you know when the time is right

and that is actual quite very true. Mum asked Sally-the-Vet to come to our house. So, in his favourite sunny place in the garden, on a beautiful day, Sally-the-Vet sent Charlie to the Rainbow Bridge* and it wasn't frightening or strange. Mum and Dad did sit in the garden with Charlie and cried and stroked him and got to say goodbye to him quietly and nicely, in a safe special private place. Which all sounds very sad but in some strange actual way, it wasn't. Because it felted right, Mum says. They miss Charlie and are sad that he did die but in a kind, happy way. There is no scaredy-fright stuff around it. It wasn't traumatic, Dad says, which means they can remember him and have happy forts of when he was alive, rather than remember being scared and frightened when he died. Mum says it's called a 'good death' and if anyone wonders why this is himportant for the peoples still actual living, Mum tells them about Charlie.

**Rainbow Bridge*

Just this side of heaven is a place called Rainbow Bridge. When an animal dies that has been especially close to someone here, that pet goes to Rainbow Bridge. There are meadows and hills for all of our special friends so they can run and play together. There is plenty of food, water and sunshine, and our friends are warm and comfortable. All the animals who had been ill and old are restored to health and vigor; those who were hurt or maimed are made whole and strong again, just as we remember them in our dreams of days and times gone by.

The animals are happy and content, except for one small fing; they each miss someone very special to them, who had to be left behind. They all run and play together, but the day comes when one suddenly stops and looks into the distance. His bright eyes are intent; His eager body quivers. Suddenly he begins to run from the group, flying over the green grass, his legs carrying him faster and faster.

You have been spotted, and when you and your special friend finally meet, you cling together in joyous reunion, never to be parted again. The happy kisses rain upon your face; your hands again caress the beloved head, and you look once more into the trusting eyes of your pet, so long gone from your life but never absent from your heart. Then you cross Rainbow Bridge together....

Author unknown

13 June 2014

All of the previously ginger one's hexams are over now which is a big actual relief for everyboddedy, hespecially her. The fuge ginger boyman still has a week to go so none of us can do relaxing yet. Everyfing is going very ok for him, he do say, but then he starts to try to explain the questions and wot he did write and everyboddedy does look very confuddled. Mum and Dad try to do exerlent listening and nodding and asking questions, which the fuge ginger boyman says does helping a lot. Dad tries to keep up with some of the Fizicks and Mum does her best with the Bio-jelly but to be actual honest, they hunderstand as much as I do about it all.

14 June 2014

The fuge ginger boyman has tooked a night off from remembering for his hexams because the World Cup of Football is on the telly. Mum doesn't actual much like football but she do like sport and everyboddedy here do agree that anyfink to do with Himportant Sport has to get actual watched. Or not. Depending on the House Rules of Himportant Sport. My famberly does actual believe that if they do not follow these rules then 'we' will lose.

The actual rules are quite very complercated but I shall try to hexplain:

1. Everyboddedy who do want to watch the Himportant Sport has to be in the actual room for the start.

2. You can leave the room if 'we' is losing but you can't leave if 'we' is winning. Even if you need a wee.

3. If you were not watching at the start, you cannot be coming into the room to watch if 'we' are winning.

4. If 'we' are losing, you can come into the room but if

'we' score hafter you arrive, you can't be leaving.

5. Unless, we start losing again, in which case you HAVE to leave the room until we score again. And then you can't be coming in hagain because you is hobviously the reason why we keep scoring goals. But you has to be available to come back in again if the other team starts winning.

6. None of the rules above actual apply to the previously ginger one because she do just come to steal sips of beer and laugh at the rest of the famberly watching the telly. It has binned proved that her wandering in and out do not have any himpact on the result which is a good blinking job because trying to force the previously ginger one to watch football would be like trying to persuade me to carry a handbag.

7. You is NOT allowed to hadmire the beards of any of the players on the other side. This rule only actual applies to Mum. The fuge ginger boyman and Dad do not be admiring the beards of any players or heven noticing them. Neither does anyboddedy else who comes to watch Himportant Sport with us and they all fink Mum is a bit bonkers going on about beards. Then, she do get told off and reminded that it was her actual fault Ingerland lost to Spain in the European Championships because she forted Alonso had a fabumazing beard.

'We' is usually Ingerland. Depending on how Ingerland do in the actual sport fing, 'we' can change halfway through the competition. So, 'we' can start off being Ingerland and then when they do rubbish, 'we' becomes somewhere else in Great Britain, then when that goes wrong, it becomes somewhere else in Europe. Or not. Depending on whether it is actual France (wot Dad do not like because of, well, I do not know hexactly but it has somefing to do with sailing and Napoleon and garlic, I fink). Dad will then pick a Commonwealth country, like Australia (unless it's cricket in which case he's not allowed to) the fuge ginger boyman will pick a team from somewhere really actual weird to annoy everyboddedy and Mum picks the team wot has the nicest beards or bums. Or a particularly sexy actual player. Then, everyboddedy do hargue about which team they is supporting and why and... I do honestly actual fink they henjoy it a very lot more once the proper 'we' is out of the competition fing. When the proper 'we' is in the competition, the whole famberly does sit and chew their hands and say nuffink very much and get all stressed and tents and annoyed. Once the proper 'we' has been knocked out they do seem to have a whole lot more fun.

Which is a good job because Italy did beat Ingerland tonight and Mum did have to be sitted on, to stop her saying nice fings about the hopposition peoples beards. Again.

15 June 2014

Today is my birthday. Well, it might be. We don't very actual know so we did decide that as I was hobviously borned in the middle of June, we'd pick the day smack bang in the middle of the month and that be today. Most of the hanimals here have guestimations for birthdays because noboddedy was around to write down when they was actual borned so it's very ok with me to also have a guestimation birthday as well. Mum says Frank hasn't got a birthday at all finking about it, so she'd better make one up or she'll forget how old he is.

The biggest fing that has changed in my first year, apart from my forever famberly is well, me. I is now fuge and according to Sally-the-Vet, I'm going to get fugerer. I can stretch the hentire length of the bed and now it's getting hot, Dad says sharing a bed with me has gone from sleeping with a wriggly toddler to sharing with a sweaty teenage boy. It wasn't wot he planned or himagined. I can easily see over all the fences now and Dad says the bestest fing about coming home from work is looking for my daft head poking over the hedge. He hadn't himagined that either so happarently, it's swings and roundabouts.

I are not pleased with the new fing in the garden. Happarently, it is my birthday present. I are supposed to be pleased and fusey-tastic about it but I aren't. I dunno wot it is or wot it is for but currently I do not like it. It is big and green and round. Everyboddedy here is hignoring it very hard as well because they do know if they make too much of an actual fuss about it, I will hate it forever and ever.

The previously ginger one gived up this afternoon and told me it's a paddling-pool-you-plonker and splashed the water in it so I could see. Then she bogged off sharpish. She says she doesn't want to be standing any-actual-where near me when I finally got the flipping message. The fuge ginger boyman did do reassuring her that Mum is off-er-'ead and I won't be going to go anywhere near it.

16 June 2014

Mouse the cat is not popoola today. When Mum was giving her a worming tablet last night she got very actual vicious with her claws and has left holes in Mum's arms and tummy. None of the cats like taking their tablets and Dad is actual useless at helping. He do whine and say he doesn't want to hurt them. He tries to tell Mum she is being cruel and Mum gives him those you-are-supposed-to-be-a-man-and-you-are-a-jelly looks and a lot of words about animal welfare and responsibabble ownership. Dad just hides with his headphones on clicking Uff until it is all very over. The previously ginger one and the fuge ginger boyman generally do be absent very actual fast when Mum mentions worming the cats.

I do fink they is very actual smart. The noises coming from the kitchen are Orrendous. There is Mum saying 'Ow, you little...' followed by quite lot of swear words and cats hissing and yowling plus the sound of the cat-flap banging like a football clapper.

All the cats have different ways of avoiding the tablet.

Gipsy turns into a spitting, hissing psycho and tries to yowl her way out of trouble. Mabel do hide and refuse to come in. Frank pretends to take the actual tablet and waits until Mum do relax, then spits it out. They do go through this actual process several times before he do finally swallow it but he has stamina does Frank, and Mum has to hold him for ages whilst the tablet foams in his mouth before he gives up and swallows it. Let go too soon and you have to fish the sticky gunky mess out from under the fridge and start again. And Frank is fuge so holding him is like holding a sheep on your lap.

Mouse goes for hexplosive attacks of violence below the belt. Whilst Mum is dealing with the tablet end, Mouse do use her back claws to dig holes in Mum. There is a point of no return when delivering a worming tablet; that moment when you've got the tablet in their mouth and you is using your free hand to massage the cat's throat to get them to swallow it. This is when Mouse do attack with her back legs when Mum's arms and tummy are defenseless. I did tell you Mouse was not nice, didn't I.

I was a good boy of course and took my tablets nicely with no fuss. Mainly cos it was stucked in the middle of a lump of cheese. Mum's tried that with the cats but happarently they is far too actual clever to fall for that ol' trick. I fink I should feel I hinsulted by this but I cannot be working out how.

18 June 2014

Ohhh. So that's wot it is! Why didn't someone actual very SAY so? I have missed 3 whole actual days playing in my epic, fabumazing paddling pool but now the penny has actual dropped I do luff it. We wented for a walk and I did get very actual hot so when we got home, I did quite like the idea of a cool dip and suddenly it did click. I can also be doing getting a drink from it and everyfing. The best fing though is I has added it to my Salt Course. Now I go from the back gate, skid across the gravel, round the path, straight through the vegetable patch and splashy-plonk into the paddling pool. Mum says I are completely trashing her garden. Dad and the previously ginger one fink Mum is actual stoopid if they fort I was going to dip a delicate toe into it all gentle-like. 'I are a stupid great oaf and manic about water, so of course it's going to be chaos,' they say.

Dad's not very happy about one part of my Salt Course though and wants to set up a diversion. It's the only bit of the garden he reckons is useful and could I, 'Geroff the strawberries NOW!'

19 June 2014

Dad is sulking because he's made a fuge mistake with a job on the boat and it's a disaster HAND we also lost in the World Cup of Football again. He is spending almost every bit of daylight down at the harbour trying to get the boat into the water ready for a trip. Dad started the job when the previously ginger one was in Opital to distract himself and the job gotted fuger and fuger and now he's not even sure he'll get it fixed before the end of the summer.

It's all Mum's fault, he says, for panicking about the keel falling off after she saw somefing on the telly news. Dad did look at the keel to shut Mum up and discovered that the keel was very quite safe but then he did start to have a fiddle and a fiddle turned into a refit and now, according to Mum, half the drive shaft is in Holland getting fixed and the other half is spread around the kitchen, the harbour and the bottom of the boat. Mum's told him to hurry up and put it all back together; she's not having a year like this one without a holiday at some point.

20 June 2014

Mum felled over yesterday. She was trying out her new boots for the Yorkshire 3 Peaks Fing and managed to hook the loopy bow bit from one boot round the hooks for the other boot which tied her feets together. By the time she realised there was a problem, I had tooked several hexcitable boundy leaps forward and Mum ended up in a heap on the floor. Mum wasn't actual that pleased by all of this. I are pretty sure it was the boots she did call wotsit-beeping-fings because there is two of them and honly one of me but I did try to look a little bit concerned. Looking a little bit concerned is very quite hard to do when you can see your bestest friend charging towards you in very actual joy. We lefted Mum hinvestigating her knee and huntangling her laces and saying all kinds of rude words and wented to play.

Louise wasn't much actual help because she was laughing too very much, but then Mum has teased Louise so often for being a clumsy numpty and getting knocked over by me, that she probabbly deserved not getting much sympathy.

This morning Mum has woked up with a fuge bruise on her knee and it is actual all swollen. She reckons it'll be fine by the time the Yorkshire 3 Peaks Fing happens, unlike her toe which is going to the Doctor tonight because 'it's not funny anymore' and 'this could be a disaster.' Mum's been sponsored over four hundred pounds to do this Yorkshire 3 Peaks Fing because peoples are very actual himpressed she's attempting it when there's no hills in Suffolk and she's got a big bum. It was a challenge enough beforehand without her blinking toe being hagony.

<u>21 June 2014</u>

The fuge ginger boyman's hexams have finished so Fizzy has come to stay for the weekend and the fuge ginger boyman and the previously ginger one did hinvite a few of their friends round last night to celebrate.

They did bring lots of yummy treats like Pringles and fairy cakes and other fings wot teenage hoomans like to eat. And vodka. Mum keeps saying 'vodka is not your friend' to anyboddedy wot will listen. Noboddedy is listening this morning because they have headaches.

Today, I has been picking up their not-so-empty packets of yummy stuff and helping them with the clearing up. I was haccused of eating a packet of chocolate brownies but this is not a true fact and I was most actual quite hoffended. Blaming me for eating chocolate is not a good idea because it is quite very dangerous for luffly boykins like me. Fortunately, Dad founded the empty packet at least 12 hours before Fizzy noticed they were all missing or Mum would have had hystericals and taken me to see Sally-the-Vet in a very actual quite hurry. We fink that someone small and previously ginger OR fuge and currently ginger did eat them all and then blame me but neither of them will very hadmit it.

Himportant fings happened when the previously and fuge ginger ones hadded their party. They did do deciding wot to call the kitten we will be actual keeping. Or to be quite very honest, they didn't decide OR take a vote so he's ended up being named wot everyboddedy did want to call him all joined up. And as noboddedy will actual back down, he's going to be stuck with it. Mum says vodka is definitely not Gandalf-Gandhi-for-short-Terrance-III's friend.

22 June 2014

Today was a very special actual day for me and Mum. It was a chance for Mum to test out how far we has come and wot we still actual need to learn. We wented to the Strut Your Mutt Dog Show and I did love it.

Strut your Mutt is horganised by Wangford Vets who look after the cats when they is poorly-sick. Mum says we are actual spoilt where we do live because there are two fabumazing vet practices nearby, so the cats go to Wangford and I do go to Sally-the-Vet at Stoven.

There were actual hundreds of peoples and squillions of dogs at Strut Your Mutt. Mum did enter me in lots of classes so that I got plenty of chances to show off. It was so much fun! I did exerlent walking through the crowds and brilliant hanging around waiting to go into the show ring. I did say hello-luffly-peoples and when there was a chance to say hello-friendly-dogs, I did approach them gently and very actual plite.

Most fabumazing of all, I did win a class. Worzel Wooface did get 1st actual prize. I was the bestest dog over 16 inches. This did confuddle me a bit because I did wonder if I was the MOST dog over sixteen inches because I was that as actual well, but Mum did say that I hadded it all wrong on that fing. I was very quite lucky with the judge-lady. She did have an actual real soft-spot for Sighthounds and did fink I was particularly gorgeous luffly boykin.

Best of very all, from everyboddedy's point of view was that I did not get upset or anxious or tents. I did let the judge-lady touch me and say hello and when we were waiting for our turn to do running up and down, I did epic wriggling on my belly, stretching out till I was 6 feet long and then commando wriggling so I could say a sneaky hello-shall-we-have-a-play-whilst-we-wait to the dogs on either side of me. Mum did let that happen because it was actual quite tiring standing around being perfick all the time and the judge-lady wasn't looking at me then.

Dad did miss it all because he was fixing the boat in the harbour so when we did come home we did have to show him the photos and the films Fizzy and the previously ginger one did take and do talking about it all evening.

Everyboddedy do now hagree that I are fishally fabumazing and I do has to hagree with them. After-very--all, I has a rosette to very prove it!

<u>24 June 2014</u>

A man in the World Cup of Football is in so much trouble that everyboddedy here has forgotted that Ingerland has been knocked out of the competition. A man called Suarez did bite someone. This has surprised me actual very much because I did not know hoomans could bite. Dad says normal hoomans don't bite and he should be flipping banned, especially as he has dunned it twice actual before.

If he was a dog, he would not be able to play games without a muzzle on. Dogs wot get over-hexcited when they are playing can sometimes get very actual rough doing chasing and running, and they has to wear a muzzle so they don't do damage to their friends. When Sighthounds do running at 40 miles an hour, the odd toof left outside your mouth when you whizz by another dog can make a big rip so it is only actual safe. I do running with my teef inside my mouth so I do not need a muzzle. When hoomans see a dog with a muzzle they should be very quite pleased, not actual worried. Some peoples do fink it means that the dog is quite actual dangerous but dogs do wear muzzles for all sorts of actual reasons and most of them are not because they is going to eat a hooman. And anyway, if a dog is wearing a muzzle it isn't going to be able to bite anyboddedy, is it. Hoomans are daft sometimes.

<u>26 June 2014</u>

I did go and have coffee-an-a-chat with my Granny Mary and Maisie this morning. Granny Mary is one of my favouritist people. She finks I are super-special and a gentle-boykin which is a very true actual fact.

Maisie was nice to me and we did some gentle hellos. Because Maisie is small she is the bestest at hide and seek and can find places to hide that even if I did fink of them, I would not be able to get into! She gets into a hole then sticks her head out and barks like some bonkers octopus in a cave.

Mum has gived up weighing Maisie because she didn't remember to write down the numbers again. In my hopinion, I do fink Mum has other fings on her mind. It seems the doctor has gived her a 22 year old personal trainer man to help her get fit for the Yorkshire 3 Peaks Fing and she hasn't told Dad yet.

The previously ginger one says that the weighing fing is going to be all wrong because wot with all the walking Mum is doing, she is bound to be losing weight so it's not going to be accurate now anyway. Dad reckons, given the packets of chocolate mini rolls he keeps finding around the house, it could just as easily be inaccurate going the other way. The previously ginger one got tooked shopping, Dad had to cook his own tea and Mum still hasn't mentioned the personal trainer.

27 June 2014

We has got ignormous troubles with them blinking kittens. They is being hextremely a actual nightmare and keep trying to hexplore every-very-where. Today, Mum did shut them in the crate because they keeped wandering everywhere and she needed to hoover and that nearly ended in real proper disaster because Iris (she being one of the kittens wot is being dopped by the peoples who has just got married who is having Iris and Ivy for a wedding present to themselves) did managed to climb to the top of the crate and then try to squeeze through a gap and gotted her head stucked. It was Orrendous, Mum did say. Trying to unstuck a kitten is bad enough. Trying to unstuck a kitten whilst being attacked by Stray who was also trying to unstuck her and beat Mum up for hinterfering and scratching her when Iris did yowl was not funny. So, the crate has been moved to behind the sofa so that the door can be left open all the time, the kittens bed in a cat carry case and the litter tray is also behind there so I can't reach it and I aren't even allowed to very even fink about hinvestigating.

Iris has worked out how to get over of the stair-gate into the hall. Mum putted some wood across the bars of the stair-gate now to stop Iris hescaping all the time but she keeps having to build the barrier heven higher and actual higher. The very trouble is that Iris has decided that she do like me a quite actual lot. Mum keeps wailing that Iris is not allowed to like me yet. Not when she is only four weeks old.

Iris does not hunderstand this a-very-tall and is quite actual determined to be my new best friend. Today, Mum gived up and me and Iris did do saying a proper hello to each other. I has been allowed to look through into the sitting room before now and I has sniffed the crate hunder supervision so it wasn't a fuge shock to either of us but Mum says she wasn't taking any chances. So, with Mum and Dad and Stray and the previously ginger one all watching, me and Iris did do nose-touching-bum-licking-serious-sniffing-hello-kitten-WOTCHA-Worzel greetings. Iris, Dad says, is a cocky little madam.

All the hoomans were very holding their breath when this was happening but they needn't have done worrying. Stray was watching as well and she would have been quicker than a speeding, actual, very murderous bullet if she'd had even had the slightest whiff of me not being a luffly boykin. But everyfing is ok; kittens do bring out the Huncle in me. I are Huncle Wooface and I are feeling all very actual hindulgent and benny-volent.

30 June 2014

Because it is the end of the month, we has been playing the 'Let's Flea Treat Worzel' game. Let's actual not. Let's not play this game A-VERY-TALL. Let's play 'Do Not Even Fink Bout Flea Treating Worzel'. It goes like this. Mum does get the packet out of the drawer and I do go and hide. I do come out of hiding and Mum cracks the packet open. I do go and hide again. Then Mum leaves the packet in a streegick place so that when I do wander past she can drop it on me before I can realise wot is going on.

Hexcept I are not stoopid and I are not wandering past Mum ever again. I will do the fandango, hide in my crate, do a sharp about-very-u-turn, rather than walk past Mum.

Unless she is carrying somefing else and then she swears a lot because the one time I walk past, she can't do it. She must actual fink I are stoopid. The only reason I'm walking past her is BECAUSE she's carrying somefing so I know she can't do it.

The fuge ginger boyman is getting the same hattitude ever since I did see the packet come out because he is Mum's Evil Assistant and I do remember this actual fact. Dad has opted out because he is a big, whining, baby according to Mum and the previously ginger one says she's watching re-runs of 'How I met your Mother' at Vera's house until it's all over. Everyboddedy do know that there are about 18 billion hepisodes of 'How I met your Mother' so she could be gone for years...

In the meantime, Grannie Annie is going to get Mum somefing called Billy-No-Mates which might solve the actual problem. Gran says it goes on my dinner and it'll make it taste like eating a pot pourri to start off with but it's a lot kinder than the flea treatment. I fink I'll give this stuff a go because at the moment I are Worzel-don't-want-no-actual-Mates if being mates involves anyboddedy coming anywhere near me with a spot on flea treatment.

JULY

<u>1 July 2014</u>

Now that Ingerland are out of the World Cup of Football, the famberly has decided to support Hamerica as they seem to meet everyboddedy's requirements The goal-keeper has a fabumazing beard which means Mum can say wot she do like; Hamerica is SO the very hunderdogs that they don't even know how to play football and play somefing called soccer so the fuge ginger boyman is happy; and they do speak English and most himportantly aren't French, so that when Dad yells at the telly the players will be able hunderstand him.

Even the previously ginger one is joining in. She says she is supporting Hamerica because we has Hamerican cousins, so that kind of makes us a bit Hamerican as well. Happarently, she is completely wrong and it doesn't make us the least actual bit Hamerican so that's a really stoopid reason for supporting Hamerica. Sometimes, I fink my famberly should listen to themselves more actual oftener.

Hanyway, it doesn't matter because Hamerica are quite to lose and it's all the kittens' fault. They can all hescape into the Hall for playing with me now and I has been spending the last week being Huncle Wooface watching them playing, cleaning their bums and supervising their hactivities. Mum and the previously ginger one has been spending all their time supervising me, supervising the kittens and making films of it all because it is very actual quite special.

But because the telly is in the same room as the kittens, the hoomans do have to keep leaping up and leaving the room to rescue the kittens or stop them getting into mischief. And the tumble dryer. And my water bowl. This leaping up and leaving the room is against most of the Rules of Himportant Sport so Hamerica is doomed.

2 July 2014

Hamerica lost. But it is very ok because a man called Presidento Barmy did phone the players to say sorry they did not win and well done for playing so actual quite very well. I fink someboddedy should have told Presidento Barmy that it wasn't the players fault they did lose but it was because my famberly did not do following the Rules of Himportant Sport because they had to look after the naughty kittens. Maybe then the captain of the team would have not dunned crying.

The kittens have started eating real actual food so the smell in the sitting room is either proper actual disgustering or very quite wonderful depending on whether you is a hooman or a dog. Mum says if I do not leave the litter tray alone, I is going to be in the serious dog house.

The fuge ginger boyman has been henhancing the haroma by coming home from his summer job, taking off his shoes and clapsing on the sofa so the smell from his mean feets can waft about and make the sitting room heven more pongy. Mum keeps yelling at him to leave his shoes by the back door so that we don't get smelled out completely. He do never remember to do this fing. Mum says that Dad should do leaving his boots outside the back door, heven though his feet do not be smelling so bad, to set a quite good example to the fuge ginger boyman. Dad did point out that heven if the fuge ginger boyman leaves his boots at the backdoor he's still got to bring his mean feets in. He has a very quite good point.

Hexcept today Dad wented to put his boot on and founded a kitten asleep in the bottom of it. He is wondering if there is anywhere in this house where he can 'put somefing for five minutes without it being stolen, chewed or colonised by somefing with 4 legs.' Mum pointed to the backdoor and did say actual nuffink.

3 July 2014

All the kittens have forever homes to go to now and they is all rescue quality homes wot Mum was very quite hinsistent on. My famberly do have mixed feelings about the kittens leaving. Kittens is cute and fluffy and very actual funny and hentertaining to watch, but 5 kittens and a litter tray is actual quite smelly and the carpet could really do with cleaning big time badly. Gandalf-Gandhi-for-short-Terrence-III is staying with us which is exerlent news because he has becomed my very favourite. He do fink Huncle Wooface is super special. I do know this because yesterday I was minding my quite own business and Gandalf-Gandhi-for-short-Terrence-III did decide that the warmest place to fall asleep was my, erm, gentleman bits. He did get up out of Dad's shoe, stroll over and plonk himself down on them. I was actual most shocked but did do staying still because I is Huncle Wooface and I did not want to upset the ickle kitten. Everyboddedy did do taking photos of this as well but the photos were very quite rubbish and blurry because they couldn't stop laughing.

Iris used to be my favourite but she has discovered that she do want to be a mountaineer when she grows up and is not so very hinterested in Huncle Wooface anymore. She spends most of her time trying to get onto the lampshade in the middle of the ceiling. Mum reckons it's a good job Iris and Ivy are going to the same home, Iris is going to need to borrow all of Ivy's lives because 9 is never, hever going to be a-very-nuff for her. Ivy is very actual quiet and shy so having Iris with her should give her confidence. The pair of them are completely hidentical to look at except that Iris has one tiny white hair where Ivy doesn't. If the hair falls out, everyboddedy says you will be not be able to tell them apart. I fink they is worrying too much and there is a much simpler way to tell them apart; Ivy will the one you can find, Iris will be the one that's falled down the back of the telly or got stucked inside the sofa.

The little black boy is going to live with some other cats in Bungay. His new famberly have not done deciding wot he will be called but it will probabbly be somefing-beginning-with-B. So, the previously ginger one has started calling him Jacob. I are not quite actual sure how she did get from somefing-beginning-with-B to Jacob. There could be a fabumazingly clever reason or she could well have not actual been listening to the talk about somefing-beginning-with-B. With the previously ginger one, you do never know and it's best not to actual ask.

The other tabby kitten is going to be called Mostyn which we has been told is a Welsh name. Mum do like it very much. We will be keeping in touch with Mostyn because his new mummy will be doing Panty Mine with Mum. Dad wants to know how a complete stranger can come to talk to Mum about a kitten and end up getting dragged into the Panty Mine. Women talk too actual much, he reckons.

4th July 2014

Stray has gonned on strike. She do wish the kittens would do bogging off and leaving her alone. She has binned a fabumazing mummy but she has had a-very-nuff. She has taken to supervising the kittens from the bookshelf so she can hinterfere if one of them do get into squabbles but so she isn't being used as a milk bar. If she do lie on the floor she clamps her hundersides onto the floor and tucks her legs tight around her. The milk bar is actual closed, hexcept a couple of times a day. It do not stop the kittens trying to get to her hunderside and they do frantic diggering at the carpet to tunnel hunderneath her. They can't actual reach her on the bookshelf so that is where she is staying.

Not that the kittens actual need much dinners from Stray. They is all fat, especially Gandalf-Gandhi-for-short-Terrence-III. He is so fat her can't squeeze through the bars of the stair-gate anymore so keeps getting left out of the race-up-the-hallway-slam-into-the-front-door-look-offended-pretend-it-didn't-happen skidding games.

6 July 2014

I have gotted a sore poorly foot. It's from being a plonker in the garden, Dad says. I do have this Salt Course circuit that involves a gravel patch, my paddling pool, my digging border, (where there is a cat buried four feet down wot Mum says I will never reach) several flower border edgings, a rake wot I do keep dragging about and the occasional hedgehog. Mum said this used to be her front garden before I moved in.

Hanyway... I have somehow managed to hurt my foot doing this very normal activity at 40 mph and Mum keeps trying to have a Look. At. It. When I was on her bed earlier I did let her have a feel and there is a cut. I do not know why this is actual news because I have known about the cut for hours and I has been lickering it all evening. BUT, Mum wants to have a Proper Look and I have decidered that it is my foot, she's had a feel, I is not going to dies or anyfink so I is not letting her have any more looks or feels. So there.

8th July 2014

I just want to let the peoples in Brazil know that my famberly did do all the Rules of Himportant Sport and did do sitting down to watch the match and didn't do running out of the room or anyfink. They did just sitted there with their mouths all open and saggy and did look shocked. They is still wondering why the Brazilian peoples did suddenly forget how to play football so the German peoples could win by 8 goals to 1.

9 July 2014

Mostyn, Stray and Jacob have gonned to their forever homes and Stray has finally gotted a proper name. She is going to be called Willow which is quite actual pretty. The previously ginger one do approve so that's very ok then. Jacob is still going to be called somefing-beginning-with-B but they people's still haven't made up their minds. Everyboddedy do reckon they'll end up calling him Jacob if they don't make up their minds soon, even though it still don't begin with B.

Mum did get a message from Mostyn's new mummy saying that he has been a perfick boykin and has metted their doggy, Lola. Lola has decided that Mostyn is her baby and keeps trying to suckle him. Mum reckons Mostyn will be very happy; he's gone from one mad house to another so he won't be missing nuffink!

10 July 2014

Tomorrow Mum is going away for a few days with Louise and I will be in charge of everyfing. Or not. I are not very sure if Mum was talking to me or Dad cos we were both in the room at the time.

Mum is off to do her Yorkshire 3 Peaks Fing. She is going to have to walk 25 miles up and she keeps telling everyone, there will be Hills. I do not know wot they is because there aren't any round here. I fink I are glad because happarently they do hurt a lot and a lot.

Mum's poorly foot hasn't gotted much betterer but she has lots of painkillers and too many peoples have sponsored her for her to drop out. She'll do it if it kills her, she has said. Dad finks this is going a bit far and he'd prefer her to come back alive. She's only left instructions for the next 3 days not the rest of his life.

11 July 2014

Mum has harrived in Yorkshire and is staying somewhere called Hawes. She and Louise are very actual quite pleased with where they are staying and everyfing is super. The Tour de France did start in Yorkshire a couple of days ago and the town is decorated with all sorts of bunting and bike decorations. I did wonder if Mum had gotted muddled up and ended up in the wrong country but happarently the Tour de France can tour places that aren't France. Being hooman can be actual quite confuddling I do fink.

Before they wented to bed, Mum and Louise drove over to the start of the walk to make sure they knew where they needed to be in the morning. On the drive over, they did keep saying 'where are the hills, we can't see any hills' and getting very quite giggly about it not being as bad as they did himagine. Then they sawed the hills and did go all white and wobbly. They did go back to Hawes and make those phone calls you make when you is on a plane and you fink it is going to crash.

Dad did not do very well at this conversation. He did pretend he didn't know that Mum was having to walk up 3 actual hills and did say she was dumb and should have goned for one or none. This wasn't the positive finking pep talk Mum did want really. I do fink Dad is actual quite proud of her but he was more hinterested in talking about where Mum had hidded the ketchup.

12 July 2014

We has just heard from Mum that she did survive the Yorkshire 3 peaks challenge fingy. She had to skip one of the hills because she felled off a curb and her foot did do hexploding in agony and all the bits in her toe joint did fall out into the wrong places. So she stopped and tooked some more pain killers and then did the rest. She only didn't do about 2 miles so she did the Yorkshire 2 peaks and 24 miles with 2 hours yelling and screaming. She do hope that this is good enough for the peoples who did sponsor her.

Louise did do the hentire Yorkshire 3 Peaks Fing and did spend most of the walk singing and being Haydee Aydee but they is still exerlent friends even if Louise does know some really very quite actual hawful songs.

The organisers of the walk were fabumazing. They is called Life Changing Challenges which Mum do now fink is probabbly a clever legal disclaimer. Her poorly toe is fine but she do fink she needs a hip replacement. The peoples from Life Changing Challenges keeped doing cheering people up and hencouraging them without being actual annoying. Mum was very quite himpressed with them all and she says she could not have dunned it without them.

We is all very proud of Mum and can't wait for her to come home. Dad still can't find the ketchup, he's refusing to give the previously ginger one her pocket money until she tidies her room and fuge ginger boyman says he's sick of being the middle man. We can do surviving without Mum but it isn't very quite the same.

<u>13 July 2014</u>

In the World Cup of Football, Germany has wonned the whole actual competition. Mum says she's still shocked about the Brazil fing and the final didn't seem like the final at all. Dad was quite actual pleased Germany did win in the end though; we has lots of friends from Germany so seeing them all actual quite frilled to bits was luffly.

Mum was very good at following the Himportant Rules of Sport but then she can't move off the sofa without Dad dragging her about. She is definitely not right in the boddedy. Dad says she is not right in the head either - she proved that by going and doing the walk.

14 July 2014

Iris and Ivy have goned to their forever homes with the peoples that did get married. The man looked like he had just been gived a squillion pounds as he carried the kittens in their new basket to the car. Mum very actual quite approves of this; she do wish everyboddedy who decided to get a pet were as serious and fusey-tastic as them.

After they wented, Mum clapsed onto the sofa again. She did have to do very hard pretending everyfing in her boddedy was ok whilst they were visiting and it was very quite hurting, difficult work. Then Vera did come over to find out how Mum got on in Yorkshire. Mum tried to do some wailing and whining about her sore hips but Vera do not let people do feeling sorry for themselves and do believe that hard work never hurt anyboddedy. Vera gotted it into her head that today was The Day for moving all the furniture and foomergating the carpet and removing the 'God-Knows-What' from behind the sofa. She did not actual want to take no for an answer. Mum forted about refusing to get off the sofa but when Vera do get into one of these moods, you can heither join in or run away.

Running away wasn't really a hoption and 24 hours in the sitting room breathing in the smell of 5 kittens and a litter tray was starting to make Mum feel actual very sick. So she gotted up and after a little quite while, Mum did notice that the moving and hoovering and shoving and bending was making her feel a lot less stiff and a lot much betterer. I was not allowed to help with the God-Knows-What behind the sofa. Mum and Vera had decidered that they was in the Nile about wot it was and didn't need me being all interested in eating it and forcing them to know Wot. It. Was.

After 2 hours, not honly did Mum have a clean and unsmelly sitting room, she could do walking without crying as well. She was all very actual himpressed and relieved and happy.

So was Dad when he camed home. The only downside

Mum says is that Dad has now declared her betterer so he's not making all the cuppateas anymore. He did try to do persuading Mum that she needed to make them all to keep her moving and stretching but then he did realise he was pushing his actual luck.

16 July 2014

I are in the dog house. Last night, I did most joyfully jump onto Mum's bed and put one of my claws through the blister on her poorly toe. I did get roared at all unreasonababble like. I did fink about being offended and sulking about the roaring but Dad said I needed to be more actual careful, especially as I are a numpty about having my nails cut. I has decidered that being more careful is easier than having my nails cut.

Mum did not agree so I have just been viciously chopped and had bits of me hamputated and I are never going to be able to walk again. Hever. Dad says I are hexaggerating more than a little quite very bit. I aren't listening. I are really offended and sulking now.

18 July 2014

Just now, Mum did drop an egg on the floor. In normal circumstances I are a bit partial to some raw egg for my dinner which Mum does know, so she called me into the kitchen and said I could eat it.

I aren't falling for that trick. There's got to be somefing inside it or she's gonna fiddle with me while I are eating it. I did fink to myself there is no such fing as an actual free lunch and I wented and hid.

Mum offered it to the cats. Frank fort it was great. Mum did fink I might eat it after I did see that Frank didn't die from it. Oh no, no, no; I still aren't falling for it.

So I are now hiding in the garden from the killer egg and I is not going in the kitchen. The cats have very sensibly taken my advices and are havoiding it as well, so it is still there, going hard on the floor and Mum does say this is a Mexican standoff. She is not going to remove it; I is not going to eat it. I do actual suspect Dad will walk in tonight and slip over on it.

<u>19 July 2014</u>

This evening we did have a proper actual storm with thunder and lightning and everyfing. Mum was very quite pleased with me. Although I was actual concerned, I did stay close to Mum and did not do quivering or be having hystericals, unlike everyboddedy else.

Mum says I are to get used to storms and wot happens when we get one. She'd happreciate it if I could react betterer than the kids, if possible. Our house seems to be in an area where the helectricals do be fainting every time there is a storm; we only have to fink about having a bit of thunder and everyfing clapses. Mum says it's been like that for years and years and it never gets fixed. She finks the helectrical board should do betterer but she's not got much hope after 20 years.

When it do get to looking like we might be having thunder, Mum do remind the previously ginger one and the fuge ginger boyman wot's going to happen. They is always more oppymistic than Mum and carry on doing wot they want and hignoring her warnings. Then, when the lights go out and the confusers go pop, there is very lots of squealing and I've-not-saved-for-flips-sake yelling. Then they do run round looking for candles and spilling drinks everywhere and crying that their phone has only gotted 10% battery and that their world has just falled a-very-part.

Just like she has gived up on the helectrical board solving the problem, Mum has gived up on the previously ginger one or the fuge ginger boyman hever learning to listen to her. So, tonight I are her luffly boykin for doing exerlent hignoring of the storm and heven betterer hignoring of everyboddedy else falling up and down the stairs.

22 July 2014

It is very quite shocking finding out you is terrified of somefing you didn't know was scary. Today, Vera did come to visit and I did nearly eat her. Mum wasn't very actual happy about this and to be very quite honest, neither was Vera. It did take us ages to work out wot was actual wrong with me but now we has solved it, we are even more confuddled.

It turns out I do not like flip-flops. I do not like shoes which go click-clack when you walk a-very-tall. When I do hear this sound I do turn into barking, spiky cross and scared Wooface, heven if I has metted you lots of times before and heven if you is my friend. The sound of flip-flops is a-very-nuff do undo all the making friends stuff we has dunned in the past.

At first noboddedy could work out wot the Jesus-Christ-beeping-hell-Worzel-stop was the matter with me. Mum did wonder if I was unwell or had a hurting bit of me. Then Mum did wonder if I did not like Vera's perfume but Vera did say it was not new and she had weared it lots of times before.

Then Mum did see me flinch when Vera walked and she did say 'That's what's wrong! Wow, that's weird! Flipping hell!' Vera wented home and changed her shoes and had to do very lots of trusting Mum because she was quite very a bit nervous of me. Vera did not honly come back with different shoes but with a fuge bag of Smackeroos. Mum is not sure if Smackeroos are very quite good for me but she also did fink that me eating Vera was even worse for everyboddedy so she did decide it wasn't the moment to be reading the back of the packet. Vera came into the garden and did exerlent standing still and hignoring me. She did take a couple of steps but when her feet did not go click-clack, I did stop panicking and wented and took a Smackeroo wot Vera was holding by her side.

Vera says she's never going to wear flip-flops near me ever-an-actual-gain. And she says that she's going to bring

Smackeroos every time she comes to visit as well so that we can be proper good friends like we were before.

I do fink fings have worked out actual very quite well. Mum is phoning up all her friends to warn them about the flip-flop fing. She says it's a good job noboddedy in the house likes to wear flip-flops because we could all have been eated by now.

Dad's not sure. He reckons he'd rather I'd eaten the fuge ginger boyman; Vera's the only person who does any clearing up round the place and he doesn't want her refusing to come round any more. Mum would like to be cross with Dad about this. She do not fink offering her eldest child as a hooman sacrifice is very nice. But then she did do finking about wot life would be like without Vera. She's very actual glad it's all sorted out so she doesn't have to fink about it too much more.

<u>23 July 2014</u>

Mum has decided that all of this Gandalf-Gandhi-for-short-Terrence-III nonsense has got to actual stop. This is mainly because she do have to register him with the Wangford vet peoples and she's not telling them he's called Gandalf-Gandhi-for-short-Terrence-III. He's being called Gandhi and that is very that. Fizzy and the fuge ginger boyman are cross about this and do keep doing wot Dad calls being subversive; every time Mum do call him Gandhi they do call him Terrence and complaining that they has been hard dunned by and Mum is a bossy dictator-type person and she is hoppressing the will of the peoples and hignoring democracy. It's driving Dad bonkers. He's told them to shut up or pay the vet bills. Hinterestingly, they has decided that beer money is more himportant than principles and he can be called Gandhi after all.

Dad says in his day, young people had more gumption and stood up for their beliefs. Mum says she's wondering whose side Dad on and anyway, he is talking tosh; Dad spent his hentire youth sitting on a dinghy during the day and sitting in the pub at night. Standing up was not a feature of Dad's youth.

26 July 2014

Mum and Dad have goned a bit mad on fish for my dinner just recently. It all started when we did go for a walk along the beach and I founded a deaded fish wot was smelly and very delicious and hexciting. Dad wasn't convinced it was any of those fings and did keep frowing it into the sea hoping I would leave it alone but he did not consider the power of Wooface and well, fizicks. I are very good at sea fizicks. Dad is very rubbish at it which is an actual quite worry as he has been doing sailing for a squillion years.

I did have to show him very actual many times that stuff wot you frow into the sea does come back with the waves and the tides. Then I did epic pouncing and grabbing without getting too actual wet or biffed over by the waves. After I did collect the fish up for the third actual time, I do fink Dad started to hunderstand sea fizicks. Mum wasn't that impressed; we're all relying on Dad knowing about tides later on in the summer so we don't go wrong when we are sailing. We do not want to be doing getting stucked in the mud. How-very-ever, I will be on the boat so I should actual be able to help him if he gets confuddled.

After all my fun with the very deaded fish, Mum did buy some fresher fish for me. She did somehow manage to get hold of some very odd actual fings called langoustines for cheap. Langoustines are quite actual confuddling. They aren't builded like my usual dinners. They has bony bits on the outside and spiky bits and all sorts. I did heventually work out wot Langoustines are for but it wasn't wot Mum planned. Langoustines are for rolling on. You do put them on the floor and squash them with your actual boddedy. Then the smell gets stuck to you and follows you all around the house. I are currently banned from everyboddedy's bedroom until my fur has forgotted how to smell of dead prawns.

Today Mum has gived me a fish which is, well, more fish shaped. Happarently it is called a dab. I do not know wot I will do with it yet so I have putted it in my bed until I has decidered. In the meantime, I are not going in my bed in case it decides to do somefing I are not hexpecting. Mum is just glad I've hidded it in my bed and not hers.

28 July 2014

Mum is singing and it is actual Orrendous. Her song of choice is 'School's Hout for Hever.' She is being very loud and did make me jump out of my actual fur when she did the noisy guitar bit that goes after the opening line. She did say sorry Wooface-luffly-boykin but she can't actual stop herself from singing. It's all Mark Pencer's fault. He sended Mum a hemail about Back-to-School which did make Mum swear because it's only July and 'surely we can have a summer holiday before all this stupidity starts again.'

But now she has realised that noboddedy in my famberly is going to need school uniform or PE kit or stuff like that HEVER AGAIN. So she's dancing round the kitchen changing the words of the song wot she didn't know in the first place, being rude about Mark Pencer and telling him to wot to do with his Back-to-School hemails because she's not got to do it any actual more. There was a small pause in the racket whilst Mum wondered if she should feel all nostalgic about this but that lasted about a second before she started singing again. SCHOOL'S HOUT FOR HEVER! And Mum's very quite glad.

31 July 2014

Today I did go missing, got lost, disappeared, wented AWOL. To be very actual honest, I knew hexactly where I was so I was very quite NOT losted at all but that doesn't count, Mum says. She could not find me and did be having hystericals and it's all the fault of the helectrician from

1996. Dad did try to point out that blaming the helectrician from 1996 was pushing it a bit far. Mum. DOES. NOT. CARE. She's furious with the helectrician man and if she ever sees him again, she'll give him a piece of her mind. Dad did wonder out loud if Mum could remember wot he looked like or even his name, so she could be sure she was yelling at the right person but this didn't go down very well. It's at times like this I are grateful I cannot speak as many very words as Dad because they do get him into an hawful lot of actual trouble.

Back in 1996, Mum had some new heaters put into the house and the helectrician was supposed to put a bigger fuse fing in the electricity box to cope with the extra load. He didn't actual very do this, so when Mum turned on the heaters everyfing did go actual wrong. And bang. Mum does remember hexactly when this happened. It was 10 minutes before the end of a two part special of Absolutely Fabulous and Saffy was about to get married. Dad finks it is hilarious that Mum can remember this but then as she did point out to him, if your cupboard hexploded, the lights all wented out, smoke started blowing everywhere and you had a baby hupstairs, then you'd probabbly remember as well.

As well as getting a biggerer fuse fing, she did have to have a new meter put in to cope with all the day-time and night-time heating boxes being different rates, which is where I do come into the story.

20 nearly years later, Mum noticed that the helectricity meters weren't putted in right heither, so the one that should have been measuring at night was clickering round during the day and vicey-versy. Mum says she tried to explain to the helectricity company that sticking a label on the digital meter would not solve the problem. She'd had helectricity provided for nearly 20 years from 6 different companies and... it was very quite trying and difficult. She didn't say trying and difficult - that is me being actual plite. She did say a lot of very actual rude words when she got

off the phone. Heventually, someboddedy at the helectricity company did seem to hunderstand. They asked Mum to read the numbers off the meter and write them down every hour, to make sure that it was the meters wot was being wrong and bonkers and not Mum. Mum did a lot of deep breathing and wiffling to herself about being 'bonkers for even starting to try and solve it' and wishing she had never noticed and not caring if she had either been charged lots too much money in the past or going to be charged lots too much in the future.

So, Mum did have to spend a day in the laundry cupboard, (wot has been built since the other cupboard hexploded) bending down with a torch and writing down the numbers. At first, she couldn't decide if she should write down the night ones as day (which is actual correct) or the night ones as night (like wot it is labelled on the digital screen but is actual wrong) and whether the helectricity company (wot were not showing much more of an IQ than a brick) would cope with this but once she did decide to just write the 'blinking numbers down and let them work it out,' fings wented better.

I don't actual know if you've ever been told to stay out of somefing but that is when heven the most boring fings become hinteresting. Every time Mum wented into the cupboard, I tried to go in as well and have a sniff of the washing on the floor and to see wot she was doing. Mum did heventually do telling me to bog off and stay bogged off because happarently I wasn't being helpful, the laundry cupboard wasn't big enough for the both of us and she was cross enough with the whole fiasco as it was.

Heventually, after about 6 trips to the cupboard, Mum's job was done and she did take all the numbers to the office to phone the helectricity board peoples, so that they could work out wot-the-hell was going on. I did decide to take this hopportunity to finally get a good look in the cupboard to see wot was so actual hinteresting. I had a good old sniff and a rummage of the washing and then...

Mum finished her phone call, walked towards the kitchen, past the laundry cupboard... and shutted the door.

Because the tumble dryer was on, she did not hear me doing the woofy-yip wot I do if I is shutted on the wrong side of a door so heventually, I did get bored and found a pair of knickers to chew. After a while, the warm tumble dryer air and the 'Woo-Woo-you-are-very-sleepy' noise made me fancy a nap, so I laid down on the washing and wented to sleep. It was all quite very exerlent.

Except for Mum it wasn't exerlent, a-very-tall. She did realise after about 10 minutes that I was missing and did checking the garden gates were shut and running up and down the stairs and wondering if I'd suddenly decided to jump out of the garden and really, actual, beeping panicking that I'd been stoled out of the garden and looking up the numbers for the police station and DogLost and the Dog Warden and Hounds First and was just about to phone Dad in complete and HUTTER hystericals when the tumble dryer did stop and she did hear the sound of an ignormous Lurcher stretching out and bashing his very feet on the cupboard door. She flinged the door open so actual fast it did wake me up with a whoosh of cold air. I did fell like I had done somefing very quite wrong so I scuttled out of the laundry cupboard and hidded on the sofa.

Mum did very actual quite want lots of cuddles but she was being all red and wet and wobbly in the face so I did decline her kind offer.

AUGUST

1st August 2014

Fings is getting very tents round here. Mum and the fuge ginger boyman are doing their best not to let each other see how stressed they are and they is failing. Dismally. Every time fings go actual quiet, they do look at each other and pretend they do not know it is only 14 days until the fuge ginger boyman gets his Hay Level results for Universally. Then they scuttle off and try to find somefing busy to do. They have started havoiding being alone with each other now; it's just himpossible for them to avoid being tents in the same room.

Dad gotted fed up with it today. He did ask Mum and the fuge ginger boyman if they has falled out or if somefing has happened that they is not telling him about. When they did tell him, he wanted to know if there was anyfink he could do to stop them being idiotic and how long he was going to have to put up with it. Then the previously ginger one joined in and started being very loud about Dad being hinsensitive about such very himportant famberly fings. She finks he should be doing worrying as much as everyboddedy else. Dad says he don't need to do worrying; Mum does more than enough for the hentire country. When he did find out that the results do not come out until 14 August, he said he was going down the harbour and quite possibly staying there until it was all over. I are finking of joining him because I do not like tents feelings either.

Noboddedy mentioned to Dad that after the fuge ginger boyman gets his results, we'll have to go through this all over again a week later for the previously ginger ones Easy Peasys. I are not sure Mum is going to survive August being this tents. I are working on finding ways to very distract her. I do feel it is my actual duty.

2 August 2014

I must very actual not eat Mum's kindle.

I must very actual not eat Mum's kindle.

I must very actual not eat Mum's kindle.

Especially as I have already eated one of them... and stooded on a-very-nother. This one has actual survived but the yummy leather case has very nearly quite had it. Mum isn't feeling so tents anymore, just relieved she isn't going to have to buy another kindle.

4 August 2014

Today Merlin did come over for a visit for no reason a-very-tall as far as I can work out. I do know that Louise and the rest of her famberly were at home because Pip did tell everyboddedy that she was actual cross that she was not allowed to come and I did hear Louise telling Pip in her mostest hexasperated voice to be quiet. It was all very confuddling.

After Louise wented home and Pip did going back inside her house and shutting up, fings were very fabumazing and we did have exerlent fun. Merlin was quite actual good; he did pee up Mum's leather foot stool but he did get told no and did decide not to do it again. Mainly, he did playing with me and trying to sit on Dad whilst he clicked Uff. Sometimes, I do fink I miss out because I are so fuge. If I tried to sit on Dad's lap I would look like a giraffe trying to get into a car. Little dogs do have it lucky like that. On the other actual paw, if I wanted to pinch stuff off a work surface - wot I would never, hever actual do because I are a luffly boykin - I would only have to raise my eyebrows to reach.

Later in the evening when Louise did come to collect Merlin, she and Mum did do muttering about everyfing being fine and there being no hissues. I fink they would have stayed chatting for longer but Pip kept shouting from her garden that it was all Very. Actual. Unfair. that she was not hinvolved. When Pip do Complaints to the Management noboddedy can do pretending they aren't getting the message; it's like one of those road diggering fings only squeakier. She did give Merlin a right hypersonic ear-bashing as he walked up their path. I fink she was quite very actual jealous.

6th August 2014

It was a naudition. A try out. A test! It was to see if we was a nightmare together - which we was not - and to see if we did scare the living wotsits out of the cats - which we didn't SO, it's all fixed and I are so hexcited because Merlin will be coming to stay with us for a few days! We're gonna play, and have sleep overs and jump all over Dad's goolies and steal cat food and it's going to be fabby-fabumazing.

Maybe we can catch the mole in the garden cos he can dig one end and I'll digger at the other end and... Mum says it's already looks like somefing out of a World War One film out there and could we not.

8 August 2014

My plan to distract Mum and stop her from being very so tents is working well. Today I did arrange for her to go and see the previously ginger one's sexy hoptician. Well, very sort of. I did eat the previously ginger one's glasses and after Mum spended ages finding all the bits of the lens to make sure I hadn't eated any, she did realise she would have to make an appointment to see Sanjay. And that cheered her right up.

Dad reckons Mum chooses medical peoples based on whether they is gorgeous of not. Mum says this is quite reedickerless and not actual true but given then number of medical people's the previously ginger one does have to see, finding one who Sarah wants to actual visit is a very bonus. Dad aren't convinced; he reckons Mum is protesting way too actual quite very much.

9 August 2014

Did you know it is honly 5 days until the fuge ginger boyman gets his results? Dad says everyboddedy in the Suffolk does know and could Mum please stop going on about it. He is sure there must be a helpline for hysterical parents waiting for Hay Level results and He. Is. Not. It. There is nuffink we can do now, Dad says; he worked really hard and Mum is supposed to be setting a good example. Mum says she's sick of setting good examples; she's been doing it for 19 years and she just wants to panic like any normal person.

Dad's gone off down the harbour again.

11 August 2014

Me and Merlin did have exerlent fun at the weekend. Merlin was a very good boykin and did not do any howling like wot his mum said he might. We did play bitey-facey a lot but we was not too hexuberant and didn't do breaking the house or nuffink. He is going to be allowed to come again which is just fabumazing!

Mum didn't dare take us for a walk. She was very quite scared of losing Merlin if he did decide to do bogging off looking for his mum but we did get lots of exercise in the house and tearing up and down the garden. And diggering it. And peeing on everyfing twice. Today we did go on a walk together now that Louise is back and Pip was very actual pleased to see us both. Pip had to go to her gran's when Merlin did stay with us and I fink she was made to do granny fings like knitting and eating with her elbows off the table, cos she was running and jumping about like a puppy. Pip is not actual a puppy but is a proper growed up dog, so it was very fun to see her being so silly.

Next time Louise do go away, I are hoping Mum will let Pip stay as well. We has all promised to be very actual quite good dogs.

12 August 2014

All the running away and hiding from the Hay Level stress means that Dad has finally gotted the boat in the water. This isn't as easy as it sounds and generally hinvolves a lot of finger-crossing and wincing and panicking.

Mum is banned from going down to watch the boat being launched because Dad says Mum knows enough about boats and sailing to be annoying but not enough to offer her hopinion to peoples who have been doing it all their lives. She is no help wot-so-very-ever and she winds John, Dad's boss, right very up. The last fing Dad wants is John getting tents whilst our boat is hanging on the end of a crane, wot John is hoperating under very actual difficult and complercated conditions.

Mum does actual agree with staying away when they is using the crane to get our boat in or out of the water; she's witnessed it once and that was flipping blinking scary. When the boat came out the first time, Dad did discover that the river isn't very quite deep enough for our boat and it did nearly end in disaster. John did go bright purple and Dad did turn quite actual white and there was lots of very swearing. Mainly at Dad for buying a boat with such a stupidly long keel. Then there was 5 hours of talking about why a boat with a stupidly long keel is an exerlent choice and 3 hours of talking about why it isn't if you keep it in a river which only gets high enough to get it out 4 times a year. And hexpect John to do the crane hoperating. And if he's going to do the crane hoperating, he definitely isn't doing it with Mum being irritatingly helpful and taking pictures and getting in the way.

The trouble is, Mum quite likes John and can't stop herself getting into conversation with him. Like at the Christmas Party when she waited until had he drunked six glasses of wine and hambushed him. Before he knew wot was happening, he'd agreed to sponsor the previously ginger one for the Tall Ships race next month. This is proper, actual kind and generous but it is the sort of fing Dad really, wheely wishes Mum wouldn't do.

13 August 2014

Today, the previously ginger one did buy Gandhi a new toy. It is like a fishy birdy fing on a string and a stick. Gandhi wasn't much himpressed with it but I did saving the day by playing with it just like a kitten. I did do gentle pounce and chase with it and I made everyboddedy laugh.

Well, someboddedy's got to. Tomorrow, the fuge ginger boyman does get his Hay Level results and everyboddedy here is beyond tents and stressed, even Dad who don't usually join in with this kind of fing. The fuge ginger boyman has told Mum that if she looks at the confuser in the morning before he wakes up, he will kill her. Usually when hoomans say scary fings like this it is hobvious they don't mean it but tonight I are not so sure.

To make sure Mum is still alive by tomorrow evening, the fuge ginger boyman has made a plan and Mum is to stick to it. Or else. He and Mum will get up at seven o'clock and Mum will make a cuppatea. Whilst she is doing this, the fuge ginger boyman will look on the confuser without Mum being in the room to see if there is any hinformation from the Universally. Then he will show Mum and then they will go to school to collect the results. And Mum will stay in the car. And not hinterfere.

Dad says he'd better do well cos the fuge ginger boyman has finished off all his own halcohol and there is only Dad's whiskery left.

14 August 2014 - very too early

The planning and the death threats from the fuge ginger boyman did end up being hunnecessary. It did all get screwed up by a text from the Universally saying CONGRATULATIONS. We has all assumed this means he has dunned well enough to go to Universally. We don't know wot he got but we know he is very quite IN. Everyboddedy is actual giggling and hugging and shouting about people who send unhexpected texts and all the tents has goned. Dad has goned off to work and isn't worrying about his whiskery hanymore. Noboddedy has remembered to give me my breakfast but I aren't sure I want it yet. Everyfing is too actual early and hexcitable for me. I are going back to bed.

14 August 2014 - later

I didn't go to collect the fuge ginger boyman's results. I fort I would not be an actual help at the school where half the people were crying because they were happy and half were crying because their world has falled apart, and the teachers were trying to separate one group from the other and be happy for one lot and worried and sad for the others. It sounds like flipping actual hard work to me.

Mum was allowed to go into the school after all because the fuge ginger boyman wasn't worried anymore. Turns out he did get more than he needed and gotted somefing called a HayStar which did shock and surprise everyboddedy. Especially the fuge ginger boyman who didn't fink it was mathematically possible. He's not harguing though.

Mum did do lots of crying when the fuge ginger boyman wasn't looking. It's been the year from hell in many ways, she says, and it is such a fuge and flipping actual RELIEF that the fuge ginger boyman did get wot he did deserve.

The fuge ginger boyman has dunned the confuser work accepting his place at Universally and phoned all the grannies and now everyboddedy is sitting around all shocked and knackered. I don't fink anyboddedy did do sleeping last night. I has suggested a walk but no-one does have any henergy left so I has goned into the garden to finish my course work in Hay Level Diggering-Up-The-Mole.

15 August 2014

When Dad did come home from work last night, he did wonder if we could go sailing now that all the very quite panic about the fuge ginger boyman's Hay Levels is over. He wasn't actual pleased to discover we has got to wait another whole week until the previously ginger one gets the results for her Easy Peasys. He started muttering about everyfing getting tents and panicky again but Mum did give him A Look and Some Words. Noboddedy is to be hexpecting anyfink about the previously ginger one's results. As far as Mum is concerned, the previously ginger one passed them by trying to do the hexams when she was in Opital. Everyboddedy is to NOT be getting tents about them. Dad did then wonder if we weren't going to worry about them, could we go sailing and get the results when we got back. Mum says we're getting a bit more tents and worrying than that thank-you-very-much and we will be waiting until after 21st. Dad can't work out if he wishes this summer would end, or whether it hasn't started yet and if he can fit all of the summer into the 3 weeks that will be left at this rate. He's gone off down the harbour to find somefing else to fix.

17 August 2014

I smell. I is covered in mud and fox poo HAND cow poo and I is being quite actual cross with hanyone who finks they is going to change this state of affairs. I is not being hosed, I is not having a bath and I is not being brushed. I has offered to compromise. If everyboddedy will just leave me a-blinking-lone, I will go up to Mum and

Dad's bed and have a good ol' lick and then wait there for it to dry off. Happarently this is unacceptababble. So now I is sulking big time.

18 August 2014

During the night somefing magic did actual happen. All the cow poo and fox poo and mud did very disappear off me. At least that's wot I are letting Mum fink.

It's really all over the sofa and the office floor but I has had a bit of a jump about and a rubby-roly session and you can't really see it no more. You can smell it just fine but you can't find it to hoover up or nuffink. I are very pleased with all of this. Mum says Vera is going to have hystericals and probabbly resign. I do not know wot this means but it's somefing to do with the end of the world according to Mum. So, she is hoovering and scrubbing and trying to get rid of a smell she can't find or see before Vera do find out.

19 August 2014

Today only me and Pip wented for a walk because Merlin did have a hoperation to stop him doing making babies and peeing up the walls. Louise says he is a little sore but 'very active indoors' so all is well. He is much smaller than me so he was more than ready for the hoperation.

Mum and Louise did say that being just Pip and a Lurcher on their walk was very like old times with Sebastian, the fuge special foster dog Mum had before I did arrive. Pip did bark and play and very quite actual henjoyed being silly like she will not do in front of Merlin.

I do hope Merlin is actual quite ok and that he is not missing his gentleman bits too much. Mum says it's all very nuffink to worry about and much betterer than him getting lost if he do suddenly decide he do like lady dogs. I don't fink anyboddedy do need to worry about this very actual too much. The honly lady dog round here is Pip and you'd have to have a death wish if you did fink messing about with her was a good idea. She would tell you to get lost with actual knobs on if you did try.

20 August 2014

Because the previously ginger one will be getting her hexam results tomorrow, tonight the talk has been all about Easy Peasys and Oh levels.

Oh levels are wot Easy Peasys used to be called when they weren't easy peasy, according to Dad. Fings did get quite loud at this point with the hinter-generational harguing and defending. In the end, I fink the famberly did decide not to do World War 3 in the end by agreeing that fings were different in Mum and Dad's day. Like being able to cheat in them for a start, it turns out.

Dad says he did this in his Art Oh Level and ended up with his picture displayed in the Tate Gallery. Only it wasn't all his own work; the man who did design the cover of a Status Quo album should have had a very lot of the credit seeing as Dad basically copied it.

Mum says she's only got Chemistry Oh level because the hexam board sent the wrong paper and she was stucked in a room for 3 hours with very nuffink to do but read other people's notes. Very clever other people's notes it turns out because she passed it. None of her friends has ever really forgived her for that. Especially the ones that didn't pass. Mum says that isn't really cheating but lots of people fort it was very quite not fair seeing as she didn't go to any of the lessons.

Happarently, the whole actual point of all this talk was to try and help the previously ginger one not get too tents or worried about her results tomorrow because she did take them when she was in Opital and off-er-'ead on tablets. She is not to worry about a fing, Mum keeps saying. If she passed them, then fantastic; if she didn't, then there was a good reason and it's not because she is stoopid. Everyboddedy has been tying themselves in quite actual knots trying to say the right very fing. They start off saying they are easy peasy and she'll have done fine but then they realise that if she hasn't passed, then saying this won't help tomorrow. So then they say they are not easy peasy, they are hard which means she will be finking she's failed them all and getting all hupset tonight. In my hopinion, everyboddedy should just shut actual up and talk about somefing else. Or take me for a walk. I will then find somefing disgustering to roll in and they can concentrate on keeping me out of the bedrooms.

<u>21 August 2014</u>

Easy Peasys are definitely NOT easy peasy it turns out. They is difficult and only hincredibabbly clever peoples can pass them. People who take them in Opital whilst being on lots of tablets and missing their actual Mum and still very pass them all with good grades are not HONLY hincredibabbly clever but super-actual-hooman as well.

There has been lots of celebrating and phoning and Mum says she can finally relax and never wants to go through a fortnight like that again. Now that all the exams are out the way, tomorrow we are off on our hollibobs on the boat with all the famberly. Mum has got Nature Diet for my dinners cos she doesn't fancy bringing my raw food on the boat. I have been promised a mackerel if the fuge ginger boyman ever gets the fishing line to work. He has been trying for 2 years and has very failed dismally so far. There isn't a Hay Level or an Easy Peasy in mackerel catching so I are not holding out much hope.

<u>22 August 2014</u>

We are on our hollibobs! This is going to be a short version of our proper hollibobs to check everyfing works on the boat and that I do actual like sailing. It is quite cold on the boat but I are snuggled up on my bed. I are a bit unsure of fings because there are all sorts of beeps and bangs going on but I are being stoical which is very good and I are a special boykin, according to Dad.

Everyboddedy in the famberly except the cats are on the boat. Heven Fizzy has comed along. She is about as hexperienced at sailing as I are so I do not feel like a Billy-no-mates newbie. Me and Fizzy are going to keep each other actual company if fings do get complercated and bumpy.

24 August 2014

We are back from my first hever sailing trip! Dad says I are fishally a Nable Sea Dog so here are my actual forts on sailing:

The whole point of sailing is to get to the pub. Sometimes you very actual have to leave at 6 in the morning to get to the pub because of tides and wind. Although there is a lot of the other kind of wind in the boat (and fings is quite cramped up so it gets a bit awkward), this means that if the wind is blowing in the wrong direction it can take a very, very long time to get there.

The reason for getting to the pub is so you can talk to everyone else about how they got to the pub and wot the wind and the tides were doing for their journey.

In every pub I did go in, I was greeted like the very himportant and special boy I are. I was also given topside of beef. In general I do very actual approve of pubs.

Sometimes peoples doing sailing feel sea sick, especially in the morning when they have been to the pub. I did not feel seasick at all even though I had been to the pub.

There is a hooman version of the cone of shame! It is when 'some stupid plonker' catches the toggle on his 'blinking expensive life-jacket' and sets the safety cylinder off by accident. The fuge ginger boyman did do wearing the cone of shame this weekend.

When sailing to the pub there is 2 main activities, drinking tea and sleeping. The previously ginger one is very good at the sleeping bit (and so am I). She did only really wake up to put the spinnaker up and go to the pub.

Leaning on a boat is very actual quite hessential. If you do not lean, you will be doing lots of falling over. I are now very actual exerlent at leaning. And mostly not falling over.

Safety on the boat is himportant. I did have to be harnessed to the boat at all times when I was above deck. I was very good about this. I also had to be lifted on and off the boat which I was epic at. The pontoon at Harwich is horrible metal grating and I did have to be carried along that. It is quite a very long pontoon and Dad does say I are reedickerlessly heavy.

Going aground is not the same as going ashore. In very actual fact, going aground means it takes longer to get to the pub. Dad says it would help if the channel buoys going into Bradwell bore any relation at all to where the channel really is. We did nearly miss getting to the pub because of this.

Finally, it may be perfickly acceptable for Dad and Sam to pee on the deck but there is no flipping way I are doing that. HEVER.

The bestest fing about sailing is that all my famberly are in the same small space and I get lots of attention and fuss. There is no confusers or tellys so people talk and do being together. I do like this very much.

25 August 2014

I are worse than the Queen, Dad says. I do have so many hanniversaries I do not know wot to do with them actual all. First of very all, I do have my birthday wot is on 15th June. We aren't actual sure when I was borned but that's wot we've decided. I do also have a gotcha day. That's the day you are dopped by your forever famberly. My gotcha day is 31st January but Dad says I are not to fink that there will be anyfink fabumazing happening on that day because Mum is always hinvolved in Panty Mine in the last week of January and so everyfing is actual chaos enough without her having to do cake.

My third hanniversary is today. Today is the day I was rescued out of the horrid back yard and started on my journey to my forever home in Suffolk.

Happarently, the Queen do give out em-bee-wees on her birthday so I was wondering who I might give a hanniversary honour to, and for wot.

I will give an em-bee-wee to Pip for Services to the Community. She do let everyboddedy know when it is 8 o'clock in the morning by barking and having hystericals before she goes for a walk. Noboddedy in the village do need a clock with Pip around.

Lola and Sam and Simba can have one for Services to Hindustry. They do exerlent management in the office at Dad's work and don't eat any of the paperwork or the customers.

Gandhi and Frank can have an oh-bee-wee for Services to the Hentertainment Industry. Since Gandhi did actual start to hinvestigate the kitchen, he and Frank have started playing at boxing matches and chase and falling off the table and landing in the water bowl all the very time. They is quite actual hilarious and do make everyboddedy laugh.

Gipsy, Mouse and Mabel aren't getting any awards or honours because they is sulking big time about Gandhi and are right actual killjoys. Especially Gipsy who don't want noboddedy to have any fun. When Gandhi and Frank are playing she jumps up onto the table, biffs them both over the head to stop them and then stalks off.

I fink I must give my highest hanniversary honour to Merlin because he is the bestest friend ever and do put up with me duffing him up and running away fast. He never does sulking or moaning about this which is very actual kind. I are giving him a Night Hood. He can be Sir Merlin and when he arises, maybe he will grow the legs that got forgotted about when he was borned.

Mum says I are not allowed to give honours to dogs just because they are my mates and that's not wot happens in real life. Dad just spatted his tea everywhere and is wondering wot planet Mum lives on.

27 August 2014

Mum has decided to pre-register me on DogLost. She says she's not planning on getting me lost ever again after the laundry cupboard hincident but if I ever do get lost for real, she would rather concentrate on having hysterics, than be trying to remember her password and find photos for a poster. I do be finking this is a very good idea.

Mum did fink of this today because she is very quite in the dog house and feels like she should actual make amends. When she did get me micro-chipped she did get given the paperwork but didn't check it carefully enough. She has just realised that didn't send the bits of paper off to PetLog like wot she should have. This means that the seven-shades-of-hell-and-trauma we wented through getting me micro-chipped at the beginning of the year has been very pointless for the past six months cos my chip hasn't been registered.

Honestly, you can't get the staff...

29 August 2014

A poem - by Worzel Wooface

I are a gorgeous boykin
My name is Worzel Woo
Mum says I am now Dad's dog
Because I rolled in poo.

Again. It was actual cow poo. Great slurpy dollops of it wot I did eat and roll about in. Mum says this is all very well but my collar is now welded to my neck and strangling me because she can't remove it in the 1.6 nano seconds I will allow her to fiddle about with my neck.

She says I do have a choice; I can get it off myself in the next five minutes somehow or we can go to see Sally-the-Vet where between Mum, Sally-the-Vet and Angel-the-

Nurse (that really do be her name, I are not making it up) we have half a chance of stopping me disgracing myself and removing it safely before I pass out.

Dad wasn't happy when Mum phoned him. He did muttering fings about 'it being reedickerless having to spend £30 on a vet consultation just to get a beeping collar off a revolting, hyper-sensitive plonker of a dog.

Mum says I now have a further choice; I can get in the car and go down to visit Dad at the harbour and HE can flipping well get it off.

30 August 2014

We did go to see Sally-the-Vet. She didn't actual charge Mum anyfink. We do fink that is because she was laughing too much to remember about the bill. Mum says I am definitely Dad's dog for the next 24 hours or at least until the smell has goned and she has forgetted how stoopid and useless I make her feel sometimes.

SEPTEMBER

2 September 2014

It is a very actual fact that I do live with some strange peoples. So, it isn't a great surprise that we is going on a hunusual hollibob tomorrow. We is going to London, the weird way round. We are going to sail there. If you do not be knowing much about sailing you can ask anyboddedy and they will tell you it is a strange actual fing to do and it is also very much harder than you might fink.

Dad says I have made it harder cos we have to stop every day so I can run around and check out the local sniffs and smells. I has already made it quite actual clear that I will not be doing peeing on the deck like Dad and the fuge ginger boyman so this has added all kinds of complercations to the trip. Dad did try to say that if we stayed at sea long enough I would HAVE to but Mum has over-ruled him. We will be stopping every night in a marina, not on a swing mooring and we will be stepping off the boat onto dry land and not using the rubber dinghy to get to the shore and we will be having dinner in a pub and this will suit Worzel Wooface very quite well. Anyfink else will be far too traumatic and difficult for him. Mum loves having me on the boat; she gets her own actual way over everyfing and blames it all on me.

So the plan is to go to Harwich and then Chatham and

then Queenborough and then Limehouse, wot is right in the very actual middle of London. As you have probabbly already guessed, this amazing/exciting/stoopid (depending on who you very ask) trip is all Mum's idea. Dad is very putting up with this because Mum has dragged him into doing all sorts of crazy fings in the past and mostly they turn out quite well but mainly because it means he can go sailing. Dad will put up with very anyfink if he can go sailing.

To make matters even more amazing/exciting/stoopid we is racing another boat. A fuge one, coming from the other actual direction, all the way from Cornwall, with the previously ginger one on it. She is doing the Tall Ships Race and Mum had this amazing/exciting/stoopid idea that the rest of us would go and collect her from London on the boat.

There is going to be a parade of all the Tall Ships in London so we should see lots of very beautiful boats. Everyboddedy is meeting up in Greenwich and there will be a fuge parade of boats and people. And me. I are very planning on stealing the show.

<u>3 September 2014</u>

We have arrived in Harwich and are off to the Alma pub where I is made to feel very welcome with bits of beef.

I have had an exerlent day on the boat making meaningful eye contact with seagulls! There were very lots of them that did keep dive-bombing the mackerel line wot the fuge ginger boyman is still pretending he can get to work. We did all get frightened that his first catch with it was going to be a bird, not a fish, so we did very hastily and panickingly reel it in. That made the seagulls heven more hinterested in it. And me very much more hinterested in the seagulls until they did come quite actual close and... seagulls are FUGE. None of us are that keen to do fishing tomorrow.

4 September 2014

We are in Chatham! Today has been a day where I have been epic.

This evening I wented for a long walk and I did see the scariest cat in the entire world hever. Happarently, it was a rare breed and very expensive. It didn't have much hair and it had a pointy face but it hobviously knew it was expensive and rare and himportant because it did also fink it owned about a mile of Chatham water front. It spended most of my walk stalking me and trying to see me off-its-land. I did spend most of my walk looking over my shoulder wondering when and where the cat would appear from very next and whether I was about to become an ex-Worzel Wooface.

After our walk we discovered a vintage car show with lots of peoples and dogs. I did very exerlent being-in-compnee and lots of people did spend their time looking at me and not the cars which is how it should very actual be. Right now I are in a restaurant proving that I are the bestest dog in the world, watching the world go by from my bed which Mum did very actual sensibly suggest we broughted along. The rest of the famberly did fink this was a bit of a hinconvenience until I did plonk myself down on it and do epic being peaceful and settled. Dad and the fuge ginger boyman was very pleased with me because the pretty young waitress did keep stopping to talk to us and filling up Mum's wine glass because Wooface was being such a luffly boykin. This meant they got plenty of chances to do chatting her up until Mum spoiled it all by singing loudly 'wherever I can lie my bed, that's Woo's home.' After that the waitress forted my famberly was weird and sended someboddedy else over to serve our table. He was called the Manager.

5 September 2014.

We are at Queenborough. Well, very sort of. We is tied to a fuge lump of concrete wot is shaped like a boat and it is about 20 metres long and about 10 metres wide. Himagine the smallest island in the hentire world made of concrete. That is wot we is on. Usually, there is somefing called a water taxi wot do collect you off this concrete island and take you to the pub but the water taxi is broken so we is stucked. Fortunately, I consider the concrete island to be land and has dunned a wee which was actual worrying Mum for a very bit.

The fuge ginger boyman decidered he wasn't going to be stucked and he did blow up the rubber dinghy so he could go to the pub and to the fishnchip shop. Mum and Dad did do wondering if I wanted to go with them. We was all very finking about this and then Fizzy got into the rubber dinghy and as she did, she caughted her foot on the lid wot stops all the air coming out. Hunfortunately, the rubber dinghy was already inned the water at this point. The air all started hissing loudly out of the rubber dinghy, the fuge ginger boyman started yelling loudly cos he couldn't see where Fizzy had kicked the lid and Fizzy started squealing and screaming and swearing.

Mum and Dad were no very help wot-so-very-a-tall. Dad was too busy laughing and Mum was too actual filming them and there was no way she was stopping as they can both very swim and weren't going to do drowning.

After all of this, I did decide I did not fancy going in the rubber boat wot only doesn't sink if you keep the air in it by 'not kicking off the blinking lid.' I are staying right here on this hunsinkable concrete island spectatoring the fuge ginger boyman's rowing efforts with Dad. Dad did exerlent commentating on the action; mainly about the fuge ginger boyman's lack of hunderstanding about tides and how he's currently heading back to Chatham faster than he's rowing to Queenborough.

<u>6 September 2014</u>

I aren't actual sure if we did get up early, or if it was still yesterday when we did leave to go to London today but it was still actual dark. We did have to leave at 4am which is definitely stoopid o'clock but we were all very quite hexcited so noboddedy did mind too actual much. Fizzy and me didn't mind a-very-tall; we stayed in bed.

The Thames is very quite long and for lots of it, you do not feeling like you is heading into a fuge city. It do feel like a very wide country river. Hoccasionally you do see large ships. Hoccasionally, you do panic cos there are flashing lights in the distance wot do mean nuffink Dad has ever seen in 40 years of sailing professionally and wonder if you are going to not see a ship until it is too flipping late. Then you do realise it is a nightclub in Southend.

All of the famberly have read Bernard Cornwell's Uhtred books and did very feel that sliding up the Thames as the sun rose was a bit like Viking times. There was lots of mist and marsh and not a lot of see. It all felt like hexploring and venturing into the unknown, which is daft because we did all know hexactly wot was ahead. London. Everyboddedy was very actual quiet and almost whispering; like we were a secret sneaking up on 10 million people.

At this point in the trip, Dad did realise that Mum had dunned her usual fing of dragging him into somefing that starts off looking stoopid but turns out brilliantly. He did shout rude fings at the traffic jam on the M25 as we wented under it and gotted very hexcited and hinterested in all the hinstructions for dealing with the shipping ports along the side of the Thames. It was Hofficially an Hadventure. Mum didn't say 'told you so' because to be actual very truthful, she hadn't been sure but she did come down into the galley to make a cuppatea with a fuge grin on her face and told Fizzy to get-up-get-up-get-up because she was missing somefing fabumazing.

As we got closer to London, the river gotted narrower and this made fings wobblier. Dad hexplained that the water was bumping off the sides of the river and turning back on itself. By the time we got to the City itself, it was a choppy, sloppy bumpy old ride, much jigglier than the sea which is not wot you would actual expect.

We started to see lots of Tall Ships moored along the Thames from Woolwich. Some of these were very actual ignormous and we were all very himpressed that they had mostly been sailed by peoples not older than 21. The previously ginger one was on one of the smallest ships which was moored up right outside Greenwich.

I don't know if you can himagine wot it did feel like sailing up to Greenwich in our little 34ft boat and pulling up alongside a bunch of historic and booful ships outside the most hincredibabble palace BUT himagine turning up for tea with the Queen in your wellies and you might be somewhere close to how we did all feel. The story had gotted around the Tall Ships fleet that the previously ginger one was being picked up by sailing boat, rather than by car and lots of people did wave and want to say hello and point and look. The previously ginger one was down below (wot sailing people do call it when you is inside the boat) when we arrived and noboddedy could find her. Mum was worried that all the attention was too much and she was hiding and hembarrassed. We had to do very lots of bobbing and not banging into priceless ships wot are irreplaceable, whilst they did find her.

Finally she did appear and waved and everyboddedy was frilled and excited and shouting 'Where WERE you?' It was only hours later we did find out she was on the loo which isn't very romantic or actual convenient to my story but that was why she wasn't waiting all excited and hexpectant!

After we had founded the previously ginger one and bobbed about for the bit and getted in the general way of the hentire shipping traffic of the City of London, we did decide we had caused enough chaos and wented to park our boat.

I did discover at this point that there is somefing called algee. Algee looks like very bright green grass but actual isn't. Limehouse Marina is almost hentirely coated in this bright-green-grass-that-isn't-grass and Mum did have to do very lots of showing me that I could not be hexpecting to do walking on it for more than about one second. In normal circumstances, I would have very not minded discovering that there was water hunder the bright-green-grass-that-isn't-grass but Mum said she didn't fancy me bringing it all into the boat which has a downstairs of 10 feet by 6 feet shared by 4 peoples and all their stuff. And shaking everywhere. Fings, were already a bit ripe and grubby down there already without me adding to it.

In amongst the bright-green-grass-that-isn't-grass there was somefing called swans. Swans is like cats I do fink; they is always on the lookout for food; they is very quite nosey and they do actual hiss, just like the cats do when I get too close. The fuge ginger boyman did say, as he frantically grabbed my collar and dragged me back, that is where the similartrees do end; they has got fuge snapping beaks and 'will break your oafing neck if you aren't careful.' Fortunately, I did do my bestest cautious and careful luffly boykin greetings and did not do getting my neck brocked.

Limehouse Marina is surrounded by actual very tall buildings so after the noise and tide and wind and banging about on the Thames, everyfing wented very quiet and still. It was like sitting on a duck pond in the middle of a wood. Dad did work out that £36 pounds for four people for a night in the middle of London was probabbly the cheapest anyboddedy in the hentire city would ever pay. Everyboddedy was very quite actual himpressed and promptly wented to sleep because they were very actual quite knackered from their morning's hadventure.

You might actual fink that my day ended then because that is probabbly more than a-very-nuff hadventure for a one day but you would be actual wrong. After everyboddedy had dunned having a nap, we did go on an epic walk along the edge of the Thames and watched all the boats. Then we did go hunder the Thames, along with about a squillion peoples, through the Greenwich Foot Tunnel. All through the tunnel I did get looks and smiles and I did start to wonder if they do have dogs in London because everyboddedy seemed very actual surprised to see me. Mum said it felt like we were walking a goat or a donkey through the City. We had to walk up a fuge winding staircase to get up to the Park grounds and Mum and Dad did do taking turns in letting me drag them up.

At Greenwich Park we did watch a fabumazing parade of all the people's who had sailed in the Tall Ships from Cornwall. We did waving to the previously ginger one who was dressed as a princess (but a very actual quite grubby princess if you did look carefully because she had binned sailing non-stop for a week without no bath or showering stuff) Also there were 3 ignormous lobsters wot I did find quite very actual alarming but I was my bestest Worzel Wooface and didn't do screaming and running away - unlike several small peoples who was actual very quite horrified by them.

There was epic fabumazing grass at the Park. You might not fink grass is fabumazing but when you has been stucked on a boat or on a concrete island or surround by bright-green-grass-that-isn't-grass for 2 days, finding some of the real stuff to have a roll and a wriggle and a stretch on, is the bestest fing actual hever.

And after all of very that, THEN I did get on the DLR which so was crowded that Mum had to sit on the floor and I did sit on her whilst I chatted to a lady who was very hinterested in hearing about my hadventures. Everyboddedy has said I have been a stupendously exerlent boykin and now I is wondering wot I should do with all the brownie points Mum says I has earned.

7 September 2014

Dad and the fuge ginger boyman have set sail for a very

quick blast to cheap beer and Belgium but me, Mum, Fizzy and the previously ginger one are heading back to Suffolk on a train. The girls decided to spend the time waiting for the train in somefing called Primark but me and Mum did very actual opt out of that hexperience! Instead, we decidered to check out the Olympic Park wot is huge and a bit very dangerous I do fink. There is a river wot runs through it but we did come across it quite actual suddenly. Mum had an art attack because I screeched round a corner ahead of her and there it was. In normal actual circumstances me hending up in a river is not a actual disaster but this one was about 6 feet down with straight edges where it has been builded by peoples and not by the Earth. Fortunately, when Mum did yell 'STOP,' I did do STOP! in time but Mum founded out that if I hadded falled in, she would have jumped in after me. She do know this isn't wot you are supposed to do and is trying to give herself a talking to, but she now knows she wouldn't be able to stop herself.

To cheer Mum up before we gotted on the Tube after her nasty shock with the river, she decidered we would have an ice-cream as a treat. That was her very plan but I did have different actual hideas. Ice Cream is scary stuff and I aren't eating it no matter wot you say. I also do not be wanting it left in front of me until I stop-being-so-silly. In the end Mum had to pick it up because I was being so actual reedickerless that she could not eat hers and it started to dribble all down her arms.

Mum says it isn't reasonababble for a luffly boykin like me to go on a boat, through a tunnel, up a metal spiral staircase, on the DLR and a tube and then on a train and then in the car home and not bat a very quite hiball at any of it but have actual hab-dabs about an Ice Cream. I has been declared hunfathomababble. Hincredible but hunfathomababble.

8 September 2014

I'm having a duvet day. I aren't moving. I has dunned a-very-nuff moving in the last week for at least a actual year.

11 September 2014

Today I are being a pirate. Or a member of a 1980s boyband. I are not sure which but I have 2 fuge earring burrs caught in my ear feathers and I fancy keeping them that way. Mum has other plans and Wants. To. Get. Them. Out. I are havoiding being in the same room as her now. I is having a teenage rebellion and I are wearing wot I want, fank you very much.

13 September 2014

I are not wearing earrings any more. When we were down at the harbour I was very distracted by all the sights and sounds and whilst Dad was doing yacking for hever with a man and a whippet about some weird bit of a boat, Mum managed to unpick them.

We also did go sailing for wot we fort was going to be a nice bit of sunbathing but it did turn very bouncy. As a very quite bonus, we did see a porpoise. Well, to be actual honest, I didn't see a porpoise, Dad did. And then he spended the next 20 minutes seeing it again and again and annoying Mum because she couldn't spot it.

14 September 2014

The previously ginger one had a small party last night to celebrate being 17. Teenage parties are very strange. Someone did some magic which meant everyone talked very loudly. They also did somefing to the gravity in the house because everyone found it difficult to stand up without falling over.

The fuge ginger boyman is in the dog house for not following Mum's one very actual rule: no drinking games. This meant that somebodded has gone home with permanent marker on their face.

All in all, Mum is quite cheerful despite the marker pen and the mess because she reckons she has one 18th and two 21sts to go. She's hoping that by the time the previously ginger one is ready for a 21st, the fuge ginger boyman won't be such a bad influence any more. Then she did remember Dad's fortieth and now she isn't so actual sure.

Everyone is walking round like very actual zombies this morning and Dad has taken refuge in the shed. There are far too many young female peoples wandering around the house with not enough clothes on for Dad to have hanywhere safe to look. I are finking I might be very actual joining him.

17 September 2014

Over the last few days, Mum has binned a bit ermotional. One minute she is all actual tearful, then she is all hexasperated and then she is happy and then she is cross. The fuge ginger boyman is going off to Universally but Mum's not sure she's ready for him to leave home after all.

And then the fuge ginger boyman says 'Mum, where's my shoes,' and leaves the kitchen in a state of hapocalips and Mum remembers it is a good fing he is leaving home after all. Until she starts looking of photos of him as a baby or somefing and then she gets all wobbly and wants to give him a hug. Sometimes the fuge ginger boyman gives in to the hugging but sometimes he just wants to watch Netflix or raid the larder and gets fed up with Mum being all soppy.

Dad says he isn't feeling soppy about the fuge ginger boyman going to Universally. He wants the sofa back. And for there to be milk in the fridge. And a bit of bandwidth available for the rest of the famberly. And the toilet not being constantly blocked.

Mum's not speaking to Dad now and he doesn't

hunderstand why. He forted he was helping Mum to look forward to the fuge ginger boyman leaving home but it turns out Dad is a heartless beast who obviously can't wait to kick her baby out of the nest. Told you she was being ermotional.

19 September 2014

Tomorrow is the Big Day for the fuge ginger boyman. Mum has gotted over the soppiness. True to form, the fuge ginger boyman has lost everyfing Mum has sorted out for him and if she hears the words 'where did I leave my' or 'Muuuuum' and one more time I fink she will do hiding in the larder and changing her name and not telling anyone wot it is.

I will miss my fellow scruff bag grubby mud monster very much. He hunderstands my love of mud betterer than anyboddedy else. Fizzy will also be missing him very actual much too. She is not going to down the Universally with us. Mum says she is very sorry but she needs to do her own crying and being rubbish and won't be able to do that if she has to keep everyfing together and pretend she is fine so that Fizzy don't do crying and feeling rubbish. I don't fink Fizzy hunderstands this but fortunately Fizzy's Mum does, so that's made fings a bit easier.

Dad is wondering how we are going to fit everyfing into the very actual new car especially as I are going as well to make sure everyfing is ok. I will also be taking some Suffolk mud down in the car with me. My plan is to jump all over the fuge ginger boyman's bed when I do get there so that he does not forget me.

20 September 2014

No-one said the fuge ginger boyman was going to very actual Hogwarts. AND he's got a round room as well! I is quite very himpressed. He has goned to Royal Holloway down near London and it is like a fuge castle with lots of trees and pretty ladies. Dad says it's fine to mention the trees to Fizzy but probabbly best to sketch round the pretty ladies bit. Checking into Universally isn't like wot it was like in Mum's day. When Mum wented to Universally she got dropped off at Halls and that was very that. The fuge ginger boyman did have to show his passport and do hendless paperwork and it was very quite scary in case anyfink was forgotted and Mum was very glad she was there in case somefing was wrong or misunderstood. Then there was a reception for all the parents. Helicopter parents, Dad says they are called, like wot Mum is; those parents who hover about near their children and never let them actual grow up and leave home and can we Go. Home. Now. He's. Fine.

Mum reckons she is quite right to have stayed to make sure he was very alright; Dad hadded to stay outside looking after me when Mum and the fuge ginger boyman was going through all the paperwork and it was quite hintimidating and she doesn't fink she'd have been able to do it all on her very own when she was 19. Once it was all dunned, we did helping the fuge ginger boyman get all his stuff up to his round room. Luckily, he arrived before his room-mate did so he gotted to choose the bestest bed. I wanted to help with that bit. I are exerlent at testing beds but I wasn't allowed into the bedrooms.

On the way home in the car, all the talking was about the fuge ginger boyman's room-mate. According to the room-list, he will be sharing a room with someone called Carole. We is sure we shan't be telling Fizzy about that because hotherwise all very hell is going to break out quite actual soon. We has all been trying to work out if Carole is a boy's name in a different part of the world. It must be, mustn't it? He can't really, actual very be sharing with a girl person, can he? Mum says you can't be sure; everyfing was so very different to her day, who knows wot else has changed.

21 September 2014

Carole isn't a girl. He isn't even called Carole. He's called Patrick and everyboddedy is now wondering who Carole is and if she is actual lost somewhere or secretly sleeping hunder the bed. Patrick is trying quite very hard to make sure he do not end up being called Carole for the next 3 years. Patrick should be grateful; Mum's friend Lisa still gets called Slimey after 30 years because when they were at school together someone mis-heard wot she was called. Carole is definitely getting away lightly, she reckons.

24 September 2014

On our walk today, Louise, Pip's Mum, kept calling 'Pip, Pip, Pip' and Pip did very actual ignore her.

Then Louise did call 'Merlin' which was a very actual trick by Louise because Merlin was already on a lead. How-very-ever, Pip does know that Merlin being a baby does still sometimes get a treat when he comes quickly, so Pip came running over as quick as a flash.

Mum and Louise are still trying to work out who exactly has tricked who. I do fink that Pip did an exerlent demonstration of 'How to Train Your Hooman'.

When I grow up I want to be as very actual clever as Pip.

26 September 2014

Mum did go out for an Indian meal tonight. I did have a chew on her Kindle again. I has losted count of how many I have destroyed now. I fink Mum might finally have learned that keeping an helectronic device in a yummy leather case is not a great idea. Especially if you leave your bedroom door open. And did not take me for a walk because it was chilly.

29 September 2014

This morning Mum did get a very early phone call from Louise. Overnight Merlin did raid Louise's handbag and founded a packet of Ibuprofen wot he did decide to eat because they taste sweet and yummy. Louise did want to know if it was actual serious and if a visit to Sally-the-Vet was called for. Mum did say yes loudly and several different urgent ways.

Merlin is at the Hotel de Stoven Hall now. I do hope my bestest friend is going to be alright. We are all worried and finking about him lots.

30 September 2014

Merlin is very actual definitely quite poorly-sick. He is having to stay with Sally-the-Vet and he's got a tube stucked into his leg putting medicine into him. Ibuprofen is definitely not good for dogs, especially if you is a numpty and eat 16 of them and also happen to be the smallest Lurcher in the whole wide world.

He is being an exerlent boykin like wot I has teached him and Louise says everyboddedy at Stoven Hall has falled in love with him. He isn't 'out of the actual woods' yet because Ibuprofen is sneaky. It can look like everyfing is going to be ok and then bits of your hinsides start to fall apart. None of us wants Merlin's hinsides to fall apart because he do need those bits. We will know in the next few days if his hinsides will be ok.

Louise is very not ok. She is upset and concerned and missing her Merlin very actual badly. She is cross with herself about her handbag but Merlin can be a little tyke about climbing and hinvestigating and being ever so actual nosey. All the bestest Lurchers do have a naughty streak; it's just really hunfortunate for Louise and Merlin that he did do being nosey and naughty in Louise's handbag. And then find somefing he should very not.

OCTOBER

1 October 2014

According to Dad, the most himportant fing in the whole wide world is to 'Shut the larder door!' He is actual hobsessed by it and it drives Mum very bonkers. She do reckon that Dad could actual just do shutting it himself, rather than yell about it if it bothers him that much; after all, it's the only bit of housework he's ever going to do. Mum reckons he shouldn't feel over-worked seeing as she does all the washing, cooking and worming of the cats that is lethal, dangerous work wot hobviously only a brave and fearless woman could possibly tackle.

In the winter, Dad is obsessed with the larder door being lefted hopen because it is actual freezing in there and it makes the rest of the house chilly. He can tell from sitting in front of Uff whether the larder door has binned left hopen. It's a talent honly someone who sits and does nuffink for 5 hours could possibly have, Mum reckons. In the summer, Dad is more worried about mice and I do fink he has a bit of a point about it to be actual very honest.

Hoccasionally... ok, more than hoccasionally, more like 'every blinking day what is it with you,' Gipsy will bring in a mouse wot is completely very alive and well and planning to live in the larder. Gipsy is very exerlent at catching mouses. She is less exerlent at deading them. In fact, we do mostly fink that she is running a mice trafficking hoperation, bringing them to the Promised Larderland of Milk and Honey. Well, mainly teabags and dried fruit; the milk and honey packets aren't that easy to hopen if you is a mouse.

Wot generally happens is that Gipsy will bring a mouse into the kitchen through the cat-flap and drop it, completely unharmed on the floor. All being very quite well for the mouse, Gipsy will have timed everyfing perfickly; there will be no hoomans in the kitchen and someboddedy will have forgotted to shut-the-larder-door. All the mouse has to actual do is turn right, cross the border into Larderland, wait for Dad to shut-the-larder-door and then stuff itself silly on teabags and dropped cat kibble.

Sometimes, if Dad is on one of his shut-the-larder-door missions the door will be shutted before the mouse do arrive so it can't get to the Promised Larderland. Then it is in very actual trouble. It's not in any danger of deading from the other cats; they couldn't dead a mouse if it was the last fing on earth lefted to eat. They is in trouble because they is stucked in No-Mouse-Land, otherwise known as the kitchen floor. It is actual then that the hoomans spring into action like the East German border police. My famberly is very hexpert at catching lives mices wot Gipsy do bring in. Usually, they can corner the mouse and get it out of the house within about 30 seconds. You would be able to as well if you had as much practice as everyboddedy here gets.

If the mouse do arrive and the larder door is shut HAND there is no border police about, then the mouse is lefted with only one choice and that is to hide under the cooker in the little drawer specially designed for Distressed Mouses in Hawkward Circumstances. It's where we do keep the baking stuff wot my famberly finks it is going to use one day but never actual do because Mr. Morrison and Mr. Tesco do make luffly cakes without the washing up.

It is Frank's very actual himportant work to let everyboddedy know that there is a Distressed Mouse in Hawkward Circumstances stucked in the drawer. He does this by turning into a hypnotised zombie and do stare and stare and STARE at the drawer until someboddedy gets the message. He can stare for days if noboddedy is paying attention. He do become like a fuge immoveable solid ginger brick and heventually someboddedy trips over him, stubs their toe, swears because it hurted, realises wot Frank has been trying to tell them for days and turfs the poor mouse out of the drawer.

2 October 2014

Merlin is going to be ok. He has binned allowed home with Louise and Pip but he is still having some medicine and lots of very being looked after. I are not allowed to see him and he will not be allowed out to play until Sally-the-Vet says so. I do hope he can hear me woofling about and being actual here. When I did first come to live here, I did hear Merlin and Pip and did find it all very hinteresting and hencouraging and to be honest quite actual frustratering. I do not know if I should be quiet so he do not get hannoyed, or woofly to be hencouraging and let him know we is all waiting for him. It's difficult to actual know wot's best.

3 October 2014

Yesterday I did overhear Dad saying that I didn't do roaching very well like lots of the Sighthounds that has been here over the years.

Roaching is when a dog do lie on his back with his feets in the air. Happarently, when dogs do this we do look like cockroaches wot have got stucked on their back. I are not sure about this because I have never seen a cockroach.

The closest fing I has seen to a cockroach roaching is a teenager with a fuge hangover looking nearly dead on the sofa. When they is like this, they do wave their hands in front of their faces and cannot move their legs a-very-tall. All they can do is wail 'turn that music down and get me a cuppatea.' Mostly they do get hignored or told to say please.

Dad is definitely not allowed to do roaching when he is asleep. If he tries to, he gets poked angrily in the arm and tolded to turn over because his snoring is going to wake the neighbours up.

Tonight, I did decided to show Dad all night how very exerlent I are at roaching. As I do need some very actual space to do this Dad is now regretting his comments. I did roaching all over Dad's side of the bed and all over Dad for some of the night as well. I also did some special roaching moves which I has been practicing in private, like poking Dad in the eye with my back left foot. I also did the spectacular sleepy flop which is wot happens when you has falled asleep roaching without no support and do suddenly clapse to one side with a big flump. I did clapse to one side with a big flump right onto Dad's goolies.

At about 4am Dad wented down to the sofa to do rehassessing his forts on my roaching skills. Later on, he tried to do Complaints to the Management about my roaching. Mum told him... Well, I can't say hexactly wot she did say because it was rude but she wasn't that actual simperfetic and At. Least. The. Dog. Doesn't. Snore.

5 October 2014

Happarently, when Gandhi the kitten manages to put his head through the handle of a plastic bag and then hurls himself around the garden in blind furious panic, I is not allowed to help catch him. I fink I has binned hard done by and meelined. I has been called all sorts of words and it is all very actual quite NOT FAIR. It was Gandhi who was naughty and NOT ME.

It all started because Gandhi was doing sneaky hinvestigating of a bag wot was lefted on the kitchen table, just having a little nose to see if there was the odd molecule of food in it. And he got stuck. Cats don't seem to hunderstand the hidea of backing up. If Gandhi had dunned backing up hafter he had hinvestigated the bag he would have been fine. But he decided to do turning round to get out. When you is a fuge Lurcher like me, turning round to get out of being stucked is usually not a hoption but when you is a half-grown cat, turning round is very quite easy. Too actual easy. Gandhi turned round and it didn't unstuck him. So he turned round again. And again. And becomed a spinning, whirling, squealing, roaring fruitcake with a plastic bag wrapped round his chest. His solution to this disaster was not to sit patiently on the table whilst I did woofing for Mum to come and rescue him. He did mishinterpret my Mum-come-and-rescue-Gandhi-wot-is-stucked woofing for Yay-now-you're-stucked-I'm-going-to-eat-you, and shotted out the cat-flap, still mangled up in the bag.

As soon as he gotted into the garden, the wind did fill up the plastic bag and the bag did become like a parachute. This did cause Gandhi to lose the actual plot a very quite lot more. Heven Mum could not miss hearing the sound of a kitten having a nervous breakdown at 30 miles an hour, so she did rush out into the garden to see wot all the fuss was about. I did rush out too, woofing and leaping and hattempting to be very quite helpful at hexplaining wot had happened. After I had dunned hexplaining wot the problem was, with lots of woofing and actions wot mainly hinvolved chasing Gandhi round the garden so he was very actual trying to run away from the plastic bag parachute HAND me, I did finally manage to park him in a very safe place so that Mum could huntangle him from the plastic bag. My work dunned, I did go into the house to get a drink and lefted Mum to do the easy bit.

She's gone into the shed to get a drill so she can

dismantle the decking. I are in the dog house and tonight I are Dad's Dog.

6 October 2014

My Gran is one of them there dog hexperts. I are a dog hexpert too but that is because I are a dog. Dad says Mum is not allowed to become a dog hexpert because they have billions of dogs, no money and their cars are a tip.

Gran does sometimes despair of me cos I do not behave like wot most of her dogs do. I do not be liking balls and fings chucked. I do not much like treats and if you fink I'll be jumping over weird fings for the chance of getting half a sausage, well...

Gran and Mum have conversations which start 'Have you tried...?' and end up with a lot of sighing and scratching of heads.

How-very-ever... the big news is that Gran has recently handed over some new treats for me. These are homemade and are basically the dried insides of rabbit and tripe. I are pleased to say that I will consider doing sit for these hincredibabbly smelly treats and will even take one on a walk. This is a Major Breakthrough cos I usually just spit them out and belt off again.

Dad is a bit worried now. He spent an hinteresting time with a torch looking underneath his desk tonight because he forted a mouse or somefing bigger had died underneath it, only to discover that I had hidded one of the smelly treats hunder there.

Dad says everyfing is beginning to get too hexpert round here and could we all go back to being amateurs. It smells nicer.

7 October 2014

I have hurted my foot. Not badly but there is blood on the floor. The usual actual rules are now in play:

1. Noboddedy can touch it.
2. Noboddedy can look at it.

3. Noboddedy can even look at me in HANYWAY which suggests you might want to touch it.

There is no treat, food stuff, toy, position or situation h under which I will allow you to hinspect it, so please be GOING AWAY. Fanking you kindly.

9 October 2014

Today Merlin did come out to play for the first time in nearly 2 weeks. I was so very actual pleased to see him I did do my dancing horse himpression when he comed trotting out of the gate. I did nearly pull Mum's shoulder out of its socket in all my hexcitement. Merlin did exerlent tugging on his lead and standing up like a Meercat and then, when we was letted off our leads we did epic Sighthound bitey-facey roaring and racing around. Pip did commentating in her bestest shrill burglar halarm voice and we can now fishally say everyfing is very back to very normal and Merlin has recovered.

Louise is wondering if her bank account will ever recover but we all do fink that Merlin is very actual worth every single penny.

10 October 2014

Just recently, I have been discovering that the door to the bedroom is being very actual shut at night. With me on the wrong side of it. I are more than a little bit dischuffed by this.

The trouble is, I have growed and there is not enough actual room for 2 hoomans and a 'dirty great oaf of a Lurcher who won't keep blinking still and insists on taking over the whole bed.'

I can't even sneak up there before bedtime and stake my claim because since I eated those kindle fings, everyone is trying much harderer to remember to shut the door.

I are not banned from the bedroom; I do go up and jump about in the mornings and when there is only one hooman in the bed I are allowed to sleep on it but that only happens when Dad's snoring gets outtahand and that only happens when Dad is very beyond knackered from doing work. Then, either Dad gets fed up with Mum poking him all night, or Mum gets fed up with the poking not working and then they has a fuge row and one of them does do sleeping on the sofa for a few days.

I need to have a word with Dad's boss...

12 October 2014

When Dad did say that he would be playing an online sailing game that both he and Mum have henjoyed in the past, Mum did not fink too very much about it. This was an actual big mistake.

The fing is, to play the game brilliantly, you do have to wake up in the middle of the night to sail your boat. When he is awake and not doing snoring, Dad is a peaceful soul and he doesn't clatter about the place or make loud bangs so Mum wasn't worried about anyfink.

Hunfortunately, I do not be a peaceful soul and there is nuffink more frilling and hexciting than Dad creeping about the place, trying to be quiet at 3am. We did do talking and woofling and please-can-I-go-outside-for-a-wee-ing. Dad left the bedroom door open so I did do jumping about on Mum and then Gandhi the kitten came up to see wot all the fuss was about and bitted Mum's foot which made her yell, and that made me chase the kitten. It was all very hentertaining.

Then we did it all again at 7am and Mum very quite gived up. This was fine by me because having had a busy night, both me and Dad did have a himportant snoozy lie-in on the bed wot there is not enough room for Mum as well.

The very actual fing is... this game lasts for 9 months. Mum says she doesn't fink she'll survive. To be actual quite truthful, she said she doesn't fink Dad will survive if he expects Mum to put up with this for most of a year.

But I don't need to be having a word with Dad's boss

anymore. Dad's on the sofa until he Stops. Playing. That. Stupid. Game.

13 October 2014

Mum is missing the fuge ginger boyman but he is very actual enjoying Universally and getting to know all the routines and his way round fings. Mum says she misses him doing the cooking when she can't fink of wot to make and him harguing with Dad about Polly Ticks.

Some fing Mum isn't missing at all. The toilet hasn't been blocked since he did leave and there is actual food in the larder sometimes. But most hobvious of all is the lack of mess. The sitting room does not have duvets dangling into half drunked cups of cider, there aren't 16 mugs on the floor and there isn't a pile of dead socks rotting between the cushions any more.

It is very actual quiet here now as well. Noboddedy did realise how much noise he did generate. At night, you do not hear the sound of him laughing like a squawking parrot at the Radio 4 podcasts or the sound of him thudding down the stairs from his loft room and swearing when he trips up the clothes he's left on the slippery floor of his room. We don't hear him doing wot Mum calls his Evangelical Atheist act, shouting at the telly when there are religious programmes on, or grumbling about proving negatives and 'Just because we can't prove there isn't a God, doesn't mean there is one!'

When he do come back, he is likely to get a letcher from Mum because she's managed to blow a hole in his theory of himpossible-to-prove-a-negative hargument. She's solved the riddle of the crisp packets frown behind the sofa wot everyboddedy has been in The Nile about for the past 3 years. Suddenly, there are no crisp packets behind the sofa. Dad reckons there must be a God if someboddedy is finally going to win a hargument with the fuge ginger boyman.

<u>14 October 2014</u>

When we came downstairs this morning, Gipsy had left Mum a present. She draped it over the kettle. All very stylish like... almost interior decorating even... Mum would like Gipsy to know that interior decorating with dead squirrels is never going work in this house. Ever.

I do wonder why Gipsy did leave it on the kettle. If she had lefted it on the floor I would have dunned destroying all the hevidence before Mum came downstairs and she would not have screamed the place down and had a art attack, panicked in case it wasn't Gipsy but some psychotic neighbour who was sending her a message like the horse head in the Godfather, wondered about calling the police, realised she was being a hidiot, fort about making a cuppatea, cried because she couldn't because she'd chucked the kettle away with the squirrel and generally aged 15 years in about 30 seconds. She also would not have hejected Gipsy from the window sill where she was snoozing after her hexertions and locked the cat-flap until she's forgived her.

<u>16 October 2014</u>

For the past few nights, I have binned refusing to go outside for a wee when it's dark. I are simply taking to my bed every time the front door is opened. I do be looking shame-faced and sad and no-one quite knows wot to do. Mum is feeling a bit very guilty and wondering if I did get frightened when she forgotted to unlock the cat-flap after the not-speaking-to-Gipsy-about-the-squirrel hincident.

That night, there was a right argy-bargy in the garden. All the cats hinsisted on having a go at getting through the cat-flap and then they gotted into spiky, hissy harguments about why it wasn't working. And then did lots of squabbling because it seemed like one of the cats was guarding the hole and stopping everyboddedy else from going in. Heventually, they did let Frank have a go and he just smashed his way through the cat-flap and took out half the wall with him.

I can't actual remember if this is the reason I are refusing to go into the garden but I are planning on keeping this up for a bit because it distracts everyboddedy from stoopid fings like 'sit' and 'down.' It's hard actual work coming up with new distractions but this one has very actual got everyboddedy stumped and confuddled.

Mum's threatening to call Gran tomorrow to see if she has any hideas. Dad isn't keen. The last time she got hinvolved he fort there was a dead rabbit hunder his desk.

17 October 2014

At 3am this morning, the not-going-outside-hever-again-in-the-dark back-fired on me and I did have to wake Mum up to let me out for a wee.

First of all I did bark outside her bedroom. When she opened the door to find out wot was the matter I did run into the room and I did lie down on the bed. I gotted a little bit distracted rolling around upside down for a bit so Mum did assume that was wot I wanted and wented back to sleep. Then I did remember I did very actual really want a wee so I did do jumping up and down on Mum and woofing until she got the message.

Mum was very actual quite unhimpressed about being woked up yet hagain and having to stand at the front door in her knickers praying that I didn't set off the security light and show the world her being naked. Then she did remember it was 3am and calm actual down because there was hunlikely to be anyboddedy about. Until she realised that is was Friday morning and there was no pint of milk on the doorstep which meant the milkman hadn't been yet and was likely to appear at any moment.

When I looked over at Mum, she had that look on her face wot she usually saves for Dad when he is in the serious actual dog house and is going to have to spend the hentire weekend putting up shelves to get back into her good books. I did decide to stop sniffing and hinvestigating where the hedgehog had dunned walking through the garden and do a wee. It seemed safest.

18 October 2014

Mum says she isn't going to be standing on the door step with no clothes on tonight heven if the milkman don't come on a Saturday. Wot with Dad's snoring and me roaching and the stupid sailing game and now me refusing to go out for a wee, she hasn't had any proper sleep for a fortnight and she's had Just. About. Enough. So, at midnight, she did get my lead and a tripe treat and she did take me outside on the lead and make me stay out there until I did do a wee.

It is very quite hard not to do a wee when you actual want one and the cool breeze is wafting around your gentleman bits and you hasn't got an hexcuse for not going outside cos your Mum is out there with you so you can't be pretending to be scared of the dark hanymore.

So I did do a wee. I has been tricked and I is not happy. Mum is though; she's had her first decent night's sleep in a week and is no longer planning to divorce/take a sledgehammer to/re-home the next fing that wakes her up.

19 October 2014

This evening, the fuge ginger boyman did suddenly appear as a very actual surprise. Mum and Dad were frilled to very bits to see him and this morning we did go out and do wot we do best. We got exerlently wet and muddy.

As the fuge ginger boyman was only here for a flying visit, there was not enough time for him to make an ignormous mess, so he did make sure I was very smelly before he left and that the lingering smell of wet Rugby boots (which is roughly wot wet smelly dogs do smell of) would remind everyboddedy how much we miss him.

Very most himportantly of all, the fuge ginger boyman is happy at Universally. The only fing he has binned in trouble for is forgetting to take his keys with him and locking himself out of his room. About a billion times. This does not actual surprise anyboddedy a-very-tall.

Mum wasn't going to mention the crisp packet fing but then she did realise that if she didn't, the fuge ginger boyman would claim that he had binned home and that there was no crisp packets behind the sofa so that disproved everyfing. He wouldn't remember that the reason there wasn't any crisp packets behind the sofa was because there wasn't any crisps in the larder.

Dad reckons most famberlys talk about how their children are getting on at Universally and if they like their course and if they are making friends and have they got enough socks. Only our famberly would spend a flying visit talking about empty crisp packets and how they can or can't be used to prove there is or isn't a God and actual love every second of it. We're not normal, Dad reckons. I could have actual told him that.

21 October 2014

The cats are due for their worming tablets and Mum is not looking forward to it. She is very actual wondering if anyone has some Kevlar Body Armour she can borrow. She still has the scars from worming Mouse 3 months ago.

23 October 2014

I has just had some very quite fabumazing news wot I is so excited about. Merlin AND Pip are coming to actual stay for a whole week. There is only one ickle problem. Pip. Well, Pip and Dad. Well, really, Pip and Dad and the fact that Mum hasn't said a blinking word about Pip being in charge. I are not sure Dad is going to like falling heven further down the pecking order behind Mum and Gipsy and being actual uslurped by a six inch tall dog-crossed-with-a-guinea-pig. Dad do not know Pip very well apart from her hability to tell everyboddedy in Suffolk that it is 8 o'clock in the morning because everyboddedy round here do know that; they hasn't any very choice. But he hasn't actual spended any time with her.

Mum hasn't said anyfink to Dad about Pip. I are wondering if this is actual wise or not. Perhaps she do fink Dad won't believe her or perhaps she finks Dad will say Pip cannot come to stay if he finds out in hadvance that Pip is the bossiest doggy in the whole wide world.

I aren't saying a fing. Dad can do finding out the hard way like the rest of us have very had to.

<u>25 October 2014</u>

Pip and Merlin have arrived! This evening Dad is getting a crash course in Life According to Pip. This has been a bit of a very shock for Dad but he has binned paying attention and I do fink he will survive. So far, Pip has covered wot evenings do look like in her world.

1. You must actual pay attention when Pip do have somefing himportant she wants to tell you. If you is trying to concentrate on the telly or a phone call or stopping people die on Uff it Do. Not. Matter. She will keep telling you louderer and louderer until you do actual listen.

2. Pip likes to sit where Pip do like to sit. That might be on your lap. If you do not let her sit on your lap, then she will stand in front of Uff and do barking until you do make room on your lap. She do not care if 'People will die,' and she do not hunderstand 'Gimme-a-sec.'

3. Pip is in charge of all the toys. If that do mean she has to hide them hunder your feet and have actual hystericals if another doggy do come near you then you has to be putting up with this. The halternative is that she will pile them up in front of Uff so you can't see the screen.

Dad says he's never met a dog quite like her. I do have to actual agree. None of us dogs has ever met a dog like Pip. But the actual fing is with Pip, she is a very actual secret sweetie. She is noisy and bossy and has to have everyfing how she do like them but when fings is right she is happy and funny and very, very cuddly. I do fink she is just like Mum. Dad finks she is like most women and he is very actual quite glad I is a boy.

26 October 2014

So today has been quite very exerlently hinteresting. Pip and Merlin did choose to sleep on the previously ginger one's bed last night. This all worked very quite well until the cats decided they wanted to sleep on there are well. Merlin founded this a very struggle because he is a bit scared of the cats. His cunning plan to avoid them meant he did wake the previously ginger one up 4 times during the night trying to get off the bed every time a cat arrived. Happarently, he can work out how to get on the bed but can't work out how to get off it. In the end, the previously ginger one had to shut him out of the room because he was driving her bonkers with his whining and panickering. Pip, the previously ginger one says, was a very actual dolly angel wot did snuggle up all night and pretend to be a baby; she's in love she wants us to get an ickle-doggy-woggy-like-Pippy-whippy. I fear the previously ginger one may have quite actual missed the point of wot Pip is very about.

The very most actual hinteresting fing was Gandhi the kitten. Pip did do barking at him. A lot. But Gandhi did decide that Pip can't be a proper dog because she is too small so he did very actual chase Pip. Then they did decide to be friends and Mum has had both Pip and Gandhi on her lap this evening at the very same time. I did tell you Pip was small.

All my toys have been very played with and some have not actual survived. Mum is fillersofical about this because she hasn't boughted me any new ones in a long time and she is pleased to see me actual doing toy playing for once.

27 October 2014

Today has been edercational. We have been teaching each other our skills.

Pip and Merlin are very good at 'pleased to see you'. They do squiggling and wiggling and generally make hoomans hunderstand that they are happy to see them!

I have been copying this and today, when Mum came home, I did manage to fall over in my hexcitement to see her. Pip gived me an 8 out of 10. I would have got more but Pip tooked some marks off cos when I felled over, I landed on top of her and squashed her.

I have teached Pip how to do bitey-facey. Everyboddedy is so-relived-thank-flip-for-that because her previous job in games has been commentating. A lot. Very loudly. In a high pitched squealing, screaming bark which is Orrendous according to Dad.

I showed everyone how to get Dad up in time for work. This is my himportant work of the day because Dad is very rubbish at getting out of bed, hespecially if he has binned clicking Uff all night. With three of us it was very actual much quite easier. Pip did sit on Dad's chest so she hadded a good view, then me and Merlin did bitey-facey and roly-poly all over Dad and the rest of the bed. With Pip commentating from on top of Dad and me and Merlin removing the covers, Dad did very wide awake quickly. Mum says she is very actual quite himpressed. Dad isn't.

29 October 2014

Did you know our milkman comes at 2am? Pippy and Merlin did not know this. They did actual have very quite hystericals. We is all wondering wot the milkman heard. Mum hopes she yelled 'Shut up you stupid dogs. It's only the milkman.' Everyboddedy else finks she yelled 'Shut up you dogs. It's only the stupid milkman.' If there's no milk on Friday, we'll know.

31 October 2014

Mum reckons we're going to have a stream of frozen princesses coming to the door this evening cos it's Halloween. Dad just looked at her blankly and said they were more likely to be rained on than cold. Mum fort about hexplaining but realised that Dad probabbly wasn't that hinterested in the latest craze obsessing 7 year old girls and lefted him tapping Uff and camed to talk to me instead.

She says she is going to have to do 'managing' me because she does not want an actual disaster on her hands. She's warned all the hadults round here not to let their children come into the garden in case I are out doing a wee and get very actual terrified by the sudden arrival of a small child covered in face-paint. She can pretty much guarantee how I'll greet the hinvader and it won't end well. Everyboddedy is to wait at the gate and we will come to them.

I did very actual well indeed! A werewolf visited and I did not run away. I did bark a bit but I did not eated him or hide. Heventually, I did realise that it was Vera's grandson hunderneath the mask and hairy hands. Mum gived him some sweets and also gived me some cheese. I got very quite into the swing of it hafter a while. Sweets for the monsters; cheese for me. I quite like ghosts and werewolves now.

Pip and Merlin did not seem hinterested in the werewolves. They is actual bomb-proof about face-paint and fancy dress. Louise, their Mum, does do all sorts of strange fings at weekends which mainly hinvolves going to festivals, wearing strange clothes and persuading everyboddedy to do dancing and hexercise. They tooked one look at the werewolf, made sure it wasn't their Mum in another strange disguise and wented back to bed. I fink, all fings considered, I are glad that I do live here.

NOVEMBER

2 November 2014

Pip and Merlin have goned home today. They has been very good and we has henjoyed them being here very much.

I hope Louise finks we has looked after Pip and Merlin quite actual well enough. Merlin did miss his mum a very lot. We do know this because we has all discovered Merlin can do the best I-are-not-sure-I-is-happy-those-cats-do-scare-me-I-want-my-Mum face in the hentire world. He do have exerlent ears for doing this because they can go all droopy and if he raises his eyebrows at the same time it makes hoomans go all wobbly and simperfetic and he gets cuddles and poor-Merlin-baby-have-some-cheese. I don't usually see this side of Merlin because very most often he is charging towards me with a cunning plan of trying to do bitey-facey with my ankles or run off with my tail. Usually when we is out on walks he is being the super-fast, shortest Lurcher in the world and very actual over-hexcited and silly. I do fink I has gotted to know a different actual side to my bestest friend and did heven do a bit of lying next to him nearly very touching which is somefing I do never usually do with any-actual-boddedy.

The last few times Pip has been lefted with

somebodddedy she has dunned serious actual sulking and objectering and Complaints to the Management by pulling her fur out of her sides and leaving it all over the furniture. I has had a very good look round and I can't see any bits of Pip left here so I fink she must have goned home with everyfing she did come with still sticked to her.

I fink Pip did like it here because she did get to boss everyboddedy around. She did heven get to add a new person to her list of people who does wot she says. Dad says he has gotted the message very quite clearly and now does know hexactly how the world works according to Pip. He says it's all very too loud and hexhausting to do anyfink other than wot she says. Secretly though, I do believe he finks Pip is smashing and luffly because I did catch him hencouraging her up onto his lap for a cuddle whilst he was clicking Uff. Or it could be he was after her advices on game stratigee and how to achieve world domination seeing as she is very actual quite brilliant at it!

Mum says they can come back anytime. We all fink they are very actual luffly and funny.

<u>4 November 2014</u>

Yesterday I was not popoola. At all. I did be doing world's pongiest bottom burps. I did heven manage to wake the previously ginger one up with my farty bum. Because I are usually not a stinky dog, everyone immediately did assume I was very ill or somefing, apart from the previously ginger one who said I was making HER actual ill.

Today I is welcome in every room cos I do no longer be being smelly. People are now saying I did pinch somefing I should not have. Mum suspects one of the cats did bring me a takeaway... I aren't saying a fing.

<u>5 November 2014</u>

Tonight is somefing called Fire Forks Night.

On Fire Forks Night hoomans stand in the freezing

cold in their gardens, setting fire to money so that it makes loud hexplosions and then they say ahhh and ooooh to each other. Happarently, this is fun. There are times when I can nearly hunderstand hoomans but this is somefing I do very quite struggle with.

In our village, wot seems to happen is that one famberly stands in their garden and sets fire to their money, then they get hinvited round to their neighbours' house and watch them set fire to their money, then they do all get hinvited round to another person's house and watch them set fire to yet another lot of money. If you has had a hargument with your neighbour you does not get hinvited round to watch their money hexploding.

Now, I are a dog so I may be actual missing the point but most fireforks do go up into the sky where everyboddedy can see them, heven peoples you don't like. All they need to do is look out of the window, or if they fancy doing the standing-in-the-garden-getting-cold bit, they can go outside their back door as well. You can't fence off a bit of the sky above your house and say 'These are my fireforks you can't actual look at them because it is my money that is being burned and not very yours.' In Suffolk, you can't heven use a hill to hide your fireforks behind because there aren't any; everyboddedy can see everyfing for actual miles. If I were hooman, I would not hexplode my own money. I would find it much more fun to watch the man who shouts at small children or lets his doggy poo outside other people's gates hexplode HIS money.

My famberly does not do hexploding money. They do fink it is actual very daft. They say there is betterer fings to spend their money on and there's less chance of the fuge ginger boyman setting fire to himself. Or the shed. Or a neighbour's shed. Or the new shed wot the neighbour did put up to replace the one the fuge ginger boyman accidentally managed to burn down a couple of years ago wot had nuffink to do with Fire Forks Night but has putted my famberly completely very off anyfink to do with fires and hexplosions.

We don't get hinvited round to watch other people's money hexploding neither. Funny that.

7 November 2014

I is hoping all my furry friends have survived the fireforks over the last few days.

It has been my first Fire Forks Night here and to be very actual honest, I was concerned and hinterested but not frightened, cos I is a big boy and also everyone here is very well trained in how-to-deal with-dogs-and-fireworks.

They certainly aren't as hinteresting as the cats raiding the larder. And they isn't as concerning as when Mum plays a video of my hadventures and I can hear her calling me but then she isn't. That is very completely confuddling and does my actual quite head in.

All the cats here have been seen and haccounted for so I do know they has all survived as well. Mabel is hiding hunder the boat, hunder the tarpaulin and would be hunder the shed as well if she could get there. She is making it stonkingly clear to anyboddedy who goes near her that she isn't coming out until Christmas. Noboddedy is sure whether that's because of the fireforks or me telling her off for stealing the cat kibble in the larder. I are blaming the fireforks.

9 November 2014

Mabel had to move out of the shed this weekend because Dad wanted to be using his noisy tools and moving stuff around in there. Mabel can be quite stubborn about fings but heven she can't compete with the band saw and Dad heaving a dinghy about.

She has gotted a new strategy for getting into the kitchen without hencountering wotever it is that she doesn't want to hencounter, which is just about everyfing you can imagine and then quite a few others wot only exist in Mabel's head.

She has started hurling herself at about 70 miles an hour through the cat-flap, launching herself out of the end of it like a cannon ball, and then landing on the work surface without touching the kitchen floor. I do not know wot the kitchen floor has dunned to hoffend her but it is clearly now in her very actual bad books.

Because the cat-flap is at the end of a foot long tunnel, Mabel can only see wot is directly in front of her when she is preparing to hurl herself into midair and this has already caused a couple of near misses. Dad reckons going through the kitchen now feels like running the gauntlet or driving on a motorway when a pheasant suddenly commits suicide on your windscreen. You know it's not reasonababble or likely to get a cat suddenly planted on the right side of your face, and the chances are you won't get hit by the flying fur-ball of chaos that is Mabel, but you can't help ducking. In a car, you feel pretty actual silly ducking when a bird hits your windscreen; when you've been hit in the face by Mabel you start taking sensible precautions to avoid it happening again.

I has taken to running very actual skiddingly fast to havoid her. I fink I are hunder her flight path but I'm not going to risk having her claws act as landing gear on my bottom. The faster I go through the kitchen the less chance there is that she will be coming through at the hexact same time as me.

<u>10 November 2014</u>

Today is my Dad's birthday. He is ancient but I do love him. He takes me sailing and for fabumazing walks. He does let me wake him up in the morning and he does always be really pleased to see me when he comes home.

Like most of the very actual fings here, I was not Dad's idea. I was supposed to be a small Lurcher for the boat but I arrived and he did just roll his eyebrows HAND his eyeballs.

He makes me feel special and luffed and I hope I do very actual make him feel the same way, even though I has eated the insides of every pair of shoes he does own.

My famberly does not make big performances about birthdays mainly because they start in the morning when noboddedy is that actual keen on being smiley or talkative. Or awake. My famberly are not morning people apart from Mum, who says she'd rather not be a morning person but as everyboddedy else has opted out she doesn't have any choice if anyone is going to make it to blinking work or school.

11 November 2014

We have a weird path that runs through our garden. Dad says it's called a Right-Pain-in-the-Bum. Mum says it's called a Right-of-Way and it needs to be there because otherwise our neighbours will not be able to take their wheelie bins or lawn mowers out to the main road without going through the house and ruining their carpet.

I do not like the Right of Way. I do not like the path and I do not like the wheelie bins or lawn mowers that suddenly appear round the end of the house and make me actual frightened and wobbly. So recently, I have been asserting my own Rights. I are doing Right of Barking and Objectoring. I do hurl myself down the garden at a squillion miles an hour and jump up at the fence and generally do pretendering to be a lot very actual more himpressive and scary than I very are.

Himagine you are minding your own very business and it is very too early in the morning for you to have woked up and you is pushing a wheelie bin along the path and you would rather be doing it at a much more sociababble hour but you can't because the bin men has got all over-hexcited and have started coming at 7am. Himagine you has not gotted actual quite proper dressed because you has heard the rubbish lorry coming down the lane when you were still in actual bed and you did forget to get the bin out so you is in a hurry trying to steer the bin down a narrow path and keep your dressing gown tied round the bits you don't want to be showing to the bin men... Then I do happening out of nowhere barking and hurling myself at the fence and shoutering.

You might be feeling very actual quite shocked and wondering if your hinsides are all going to stay where you want them to. You might even do yelling in shock cos you can't actual help your-very-self. Well, THAT is how I do feel when peoples bring their wheelie bins and lawnmowers down the path.

Mum says I aren't allowed to do this anymore and it is hexcruciatingly hembarrassing, I do fink this is very actual quite not fair. All I are doing is hevening fings very up a bit.

<u>13 November 2014</u>

We is having a fuge hargument here today and it's all because of a tree in our garden. When the fuge ginger boyman was two years old, he was broughted a napple tree which was planted in a little bit of the garden that was just for him. It hadded a little gate so that Charlie (the dog wot lived here before me) could not go in and poo on the grass or chew the little fuge ginger boyman's toys. It was all very sweet and 'dorable and so was the little napple tree. Only now it isn't sweet or 'dorable; it is an ignormous-monster-triffid wot has grown even more fuge than the ginger boyman and Somefing. Needs. To. Be. Done. Fing is, noboddedy can hagree wot needs to be done so they is all harguing about it.

The fuge ginger boyman says nuffink can be dunned about it until he is home and can supervise. Noboddedy is convinced. Whenever the subject of doing somefing about the napple tree has comed up before, the fuge ginger boyman has had very actual hystericals. He finks it should be lefted alone. It's his napple tree and noboddedy is allowed to touch it hexcept actual him. Dad says it's all very well him getting possessive about it but the napple tree is trying to get in through the back door and the neighbours are having to crawl along the Right Of Way path to get to their cars. It needs chopping back and Dad says he's going to do it before we get complaints from the council or lose an eye trying to leave the house. He read somewhere about being able to frow a hat through a napple tree and he knows HEXACTLY wot he is doing.

Dad knows stuff all about gardening, Mum says and he is not allowed to just cut great lumps off it because he'll kill it or ruin its shape and then Sam will divorce us and never come home again and we might not have any more napples. At this point in the hargument Mum did stop screeching and came to a grinding halt.

To be actual truthful, our napple tree is all the hevidence you will ever, hever need about having too much of a good fing. In the early days, the napple tree gived us enough napples for us and for a present for the neighbours. But in the last five years or so, it has gone bonkers crazy and is doing over-achieving in a reedickerless actual very way. We get over 700 napples a year off the blinking, stoopid napple tree. They end up all over the path, all over the road, all over the garden... outside our house smells like a cider factory. Most of Mum's summer is spended sweeping up windfalls out of the road or slipping over on the ones that have been squashed by the cars before she gotted to them.

Then we get wasps. And hornets. Noboddedy bats an eyelid at wasps anymore; wasps is very nuffink when you've tried to hintervene between 4 hornets and 5 cats hattempting to bankrupt you with vets bills. During the day, I has to be constantly supervised so I don't pick up a napple full of wasps. At night, slugs the size of actual very sausages happear all over the garden slurping away at the squishy mess and I have to have even more supervising so I don't get a napple with a side order of slug and a dose of lung worm.

A few years ago, Mum did get a deal with the local farm shop and most of the good napples get solded down there. We don't make a lot of money from them but at least they don't end up on the ground making even more mess and smell and wasp dinners.

Visitors should know that hadmiring the blossom on the tree or commenting on the 'marvelous crop you're going to get this year' is likely to get them sweared at. Mum hurls bags of napples at anyboddedy who dares to say 'make pies and freeze them;' it's not funny anymore. After five years of very hysterical over-production, noboddedy can face eating napples anymore.

The napple tree might actual very belong to the fuge ginger boyman but seeing as Mum does all the picking napples to take them to the farm shop, and sweeping them out of the road and stopping me getting stinged, I do fink she's got some say in wot and how and when the napple tree gets pruned or hacked out of all shape forever.

Mum isn't a dog though; she is much, much more very actual cleverer. She's going to let Dad hack the tree about in any which way he likes. She's praying for a sudden frost and hoping like actual very quite mad that he manages to kill it. That way she'll be free of the napple tree and Dad can get all the blame.

<u>14 November 2014</u>

Yesterday Mum did give me two mackerel for my very actual dinner. Fish dinners always need a bit of very finking about, so the first fing I did was to bury them in my bed.

After a bit I did decide to have a go at eating them and bitted the heads off both the fish.

Then I did bury them again. And did some more finking and rolling on them and picking them up and leaving them in the doorway for people to stand on.

I had a little snooze and when I did wake up, I very actual discovered that One. Of. Them. Was. Missing. I know I did not eated it. You can himagine that I was shocked and dismayed of Suffolk to discover that Gandhi had pinched one and Dad did nuffink wot-so-ever-at-all-honestly to prevent this hawful crime.

He says it was very actual cos he was sick of the smell and could I please eat the rest of the one lefted before it stank the whole house out. Dad does not hunderstand. At all. About fish dinners and finking about them or them being betterer after 3 days and all that. But I did get him very actual back today; two times!

We had a visitor and whilst Dad was letting the nice lady in with her posh clothes and pretty hair, I did get the remaining mackerel out of its hiding place and leave it right in the middle of where Dad and the lady were going to have their chat. On the carpet and everyfing. Dad pretended that he hadn't noticed and carried on talking normally with a dead fish in the middle of the carpet between their feet. I are sure the nice lady with the posh clothes and the pretty hair did fink Dad was actual very nuts.

Later on, I did drop the fish right behind his wheelie chair. When he did stand up and push the chair back, he rolled over it so now his computer chair gives off 'eau de mackerel' every time he moves.

Dad should very actual know that if he does giving my mackerel to Gandhi hever again I will be taking my fishies up to his bed and storing them there for safe keeping.

18 November 2014

Have you ever wondered about your very actual name? Names are weird. You do not get to choose them yourself but you are stucked with them for...ever. Unless you go on X factor or somefing like that and then you can call yourself wotever you do want. If I did go on X factor I do fink I would change my name in case I maded a plonker of myself.

My proper name is Worzel, which you know and I

arrived here with this name. I even arrived with the nickname 'Wooface' so Mum was stuffed on that front too. Everyboddedy loves my name and did fink it would be actual wrong to change it when it suits me so actual quite well.

But like most dogs, I are called other names sometimes. I get called 'Oi' very loudly hoccasionally. This is when I are about to belt across a 40 acre field at full speed chasing after a crow. It's the only sound Mum can make loud enough to get through to my brain. Some people say it's my jeans. Mum calls it my stoopid-plonker-who-chases-butterflies-just-cos-you-can-and-no-you-can't-chase-a-plane-you-reedickerless-dog hattitude. So, on these occasions I are called 'Oi' and then I get a piece of cheese until the crow has bogged off. And Mum breathes a sigh of relief.

Hoomans fink that it's the words that are himportant but it isn't. It's not wot you say, it's the way that you quite very say it. Mum finks she says 'Worzel, come' in the same voice for everyfing. But she does not. I can tell the difference between 'Worzel, come' (I need to inspect your feet, ear, face) and 'Worzel, come' (I have just gotted your dinner out). When she says the first one, I do hide and then she do call me flipping psychic. And it would not matter a-very-tall wot she called me if she was in the bathroom cos I aren't going in there. Ever.

I get called 'Arggh-you-Great-Oaf' when I jump on dad's delicate bits first fing in the morning, 'Plonker' when I try to lie on top of Mum when she is in bed, 'Daft Idiot' when I recognise someone I like coming up to the door and 'Silly Racehorse' when I do dance about in hexcitement when I see Pip and Merlin. Mostly though, I are called 'Luffly Boykin' which I do like very muchly. And I do fink it suits me quite very actual well.

<u>20 November 2014</u>

I are getting as very fed up as Dad with Mum leaving

the larder door open and having to shout at the cats for stealing the cat kibble. So today I gived up and did bring the bag to Dad so he can guard it. Dad says I are too moralistic for my own good!

21 November 2014

Mum gotted quite worried this very morning. After last night's 'head boy' behaviour with the cat kibble, this morning I did attempt to go for a sainthood. I did notice that the milkman had lefted the gate open. Mum didn't notice, mainly because she was trying to be a morning person and is very rubbish at it. She letted me out as usual and shutted the door so she could start yelling the time up the stairs to get Dad and the previously ginger one up like she normally does, without waking up the rest of the village. Sometime between it's-seven-thirty-you're-going-to-miss-your-bus and it's-seven-forty-are-you-awake-or-am-I-talking-to-myself, Mum did finally hear my concerned woofing and she camed out into the garden to see wot all the fuss was about. As I rarely do concerned woofing, Mum was a bit terrified that she would find somefing Orrendous or dead in the garden but when she did see me standing at the half open gate she did get all relived and shutted the gate. Then she did get all unrelieved and said 'I don't know who you are, but could you get out of Wooface's body.' She yelled up the stairs to Dad that I had binned hinvaded by aliens and that did very actual wake him up much betterer than telling him it was 'Seven fifty, you're going to be late again,' because Dad can say 'I'm awake. Stop yelling,' in his sleep but he can't say 'what the hell are you talking about, you daft woman.'

All this 'good' stuff had Mum seriously worried. How-very-ever, when the nice man from Tesco's did arrive, fings returned to normal. I did belt out of the gate faster than a speeding bullet and run to my bestest field behind the houses and run round and round like a mad fing. I wented up and down my water play area and was being like a ballistic super-sonic little wotsit. You should have seen my cheeky, smiley face. I was sooo very actual pleased with myself and... then I saw Mum. She just stooded there. With a look on her face. That look. So - I did come back very, very quick indeedly, skidded to a halt and shooked all the water off me. And onto Mum.

Do you know she did not say one single cross fing? She did not say any good boy fings either. So I is now being attentive and close to Mum to work out if I are in the dog house or not. I fink Mum's just glad that the ghost of Lassie has goned away and she's got her Worzel Wooface back again.

<u>22 November 2014</u>

My best cat Gandhi is coming along quite actual very well with his training to be a Onorary Lurcher. I has trained him to lie all over the bed so that the hoomans can't get in and although he can't spread as far as me, he is trying his quite very bestest.

He isn't very good at bitey-facey. When we try to play this game I do end up with most of him in my very actual mouth wot he finks is not clever. He is ok when I do nudge him with my face, even when he is asleep. I do nudge him in the belly until he wakes up. Sometimes I try to get hold of his back leg and tug on it but he gets cross and tells me he is not a tuggy toy then curls back up with all his legs and tail tucked away so I can't get hold of them.

Mostly though, we do play up and down the stairs. He sits on the banisters and waves his feet and tail and I do roll around hunderneath trying to make him wobble and fall off. The banisters are still very shaky since Pandora the Foster Fridge was here, so it's always a hexciting game and neither one of us always wins.

<u>25 November 2014</u>

Gandhi is half a year old and Mum has started worrying about him doing straying and going after lady cats. Mum do not believe in hindoor cats, she finks they miss out on fings. I are not sure wot these fings are that he is missing out on, because he never, hever goes outside unless he is wanting a wee. Mainly he does sleeping on the previously ginger one's bed or yelling for food or playing with me. And he does none of these fings outside. Missing out or not, Dad says, hindoor cats mean litter trays and we're not never going there again.

Hanyway, Mum says the first night Gandhi doesn't come in when he is called, he is going to see Uncle Boris at Wangford Vets to have his gentleman bits trimmed. Happarently boy cats can get hinterested in girl cats from much earlier than people do fink and heven if he isn't fully growed he's going to have to get them chopped off. If he starts wandering off after lady cats, he might go up near the main road and get squashed by a car. None of us want Gandhi to do getting squashed on the road so getting his gentleman bits trimmed is more himportant than waiting for him to be fully growed.

I do very hope Gandhi stays close to home for a very bit longer. I would like him to get a bit actual biggerer. As fings do currently stand he can nowhere near take up enough of the bed, even when he does his very best stretching actual quite hard. He is not big enough to get his actual Onorary Lurcher badge yet. I also do not want him getting squashed on the road if he can havoid it. I are going to start hinsistering Mum feeds Gandhi hextra dinners so he can get fuge and earn his Onorary Lurcher badge quickerer.

30 November 2014

It has been raining a lot recently and I has been less than keen to go for a walk. I used to not notice the weather that much but recently, as I has dunned growing up, I has goned right off rain. Mum says she'd rather not walk in the rain either so she's not hexactly going to force it on me but she finks I are blinking odd when it comes to water. I fink Mum has gotted this the wrong way actual round; it's not me that's odd, it's water.

Water is weird because it comes in very actual many disguises. There is good water and bad water. Some water is scary and some is my favourite bestest toy ever.

Puddle water is an exerlent toy, probabbly my favouritist toy of all. If the puddle is muddy or smelly I fink that is fabumazing. I has been known to run right across a field just to go and lie down in a good puddle that I remember is there. If the puddle has goned, I will lie down where it was and pretend I is in it and it is still there.

Ditches are good as well. Sometimes you can get into ditches easily but not get out of them so quick. Mum always panics and comes and plays in the ditches if I stay in too long cos she finks I am very actual stuck. Wot usually happens is that I get out in my own good time and she gets stuck. And muddy. And flails about like a windmill, squeaking.

I also like those ponds wot happen in woods which get green stuff on the top of them. Sometimes I do go into one of them one colour and come out a-very-nother one. Usually green.

I quite like the sea. I like sailing but I do not do jumping off the boat. I can't work out how I would be getting back on again and Mum and Dad fink this is just fine with them; they does not want me jumping off either! Beaches are brilliant and I do like to lie down in the shallow foamy bits of water but if an unexpected wave comes up behind me I do jump up like a bomb has gone off and race around until I is sure it has gone away again. Sea tastes disgustering but I do like to check it still tastes the same every time I visit the beach. I have eated sea several actual times now and it never tastes any better. I will keep checking though to be sure.

I do not like baths. Or the bathroom. I did used to tolerate them but Mum says a 6 month old puppy who is quite small and easy to pick up is slightly different to a fuge lump of a Worzel objectering. I will hoccasionally forget myself and go and say hello to people who are sitting on the seat in there but I does not be hanging around for long cos they do pull that chain fing, more different water comes gushing out and I do scarper down the stairs.

I is terrified of the scary yellow-snake-spitting beast that lives in the garden. Mum says it is just a hosepipe but I fink it looks like a big stick, it does squirt water at people at me and I will not be going into the garden if I do fink anyone might touch it. I has a paddling pool wot I will lie in if no-one is watching and so long as the hosepipe has been putted away at least 24 hours ago and there is no danger of it happearing.

Happarently there is some water called snow. Mum does not know if I has met snow yet. She says she hopes I am not keen on it because she isn't and that would make life easier all round.

But I has definitely goned right off rain. You might fink that is very actual strange but you are not finking about it quite right. Lego is a great toy for playing with. Puddles are great toys for playing with. But if I did drop buckets of Lego on your head, you would not be finking that was fun. Well, that is wot I do be finking of about rain. Water should be in puddles not being dropped on your head hunexpectedly.

Dad says that I like happening to water, rather than water happening to me which is very quite clever and also actual true. So, Mr. Water, if we is going to be friends, you has to sit still and be patient and wait for me to very come to you.

DECEMBER

1 December 2014

We went for a walk on our very own today. I fink Mum fort she would be bored without Louise to talk to, so she tooked this rubber ring toy and kept frowing it. And picking it up. And frowing it. It all looked a bit strange and I was not very actual sure wot she was doing. She is usually quite very more growed up than that.

Heventually, I started to feel a bit sorry for Mum. I fink she was hoping the toy might come back to her on its very own. The toy was not being very helpful at all. So, after about half an hour, I did put Mum and the toy out of their actual misery and took the toy off for a run and a good telling off. Mum was very actual hunbelievababbly happy and squealed good Wooface a lot. I was so very actual shocked that I did drop the toy in a puddle...

Mum did not very actual realise that the puddle had about a paw length of mud in the bottom of it. But I did show her how to churn it all up and the toy did heventually float to the top.

I do not know if Mum will bring the toy out to play again. I fink she is be very quite hoping Louise will be able to come out next time. Louise is much more hinteresting and generally doesn't make Mum get cold, wet and muddy.

2nd December 2014

It seems like the rubber ring playing is a much actual very biggerer deal than I did realise. Happarently, after 11 months, I has really quite FINALLY dunned playing with Mum. And happarently this is a good fing and A Step in the Right Direction.

I has got no hidea wot they is all going on about or why it is so himportant or frilling but I don't see no reason not to do it again if it's going to keep Mum very quite happy. I'll even actual do it tomorrow if she likes.

3rd December 2014

Mum likes. She likes a lot. She is frilled to bits when I do playing with her. Heven betterer, since I has started picking up the rubber ring and very sometimes bringing it back, the word 'sit' has not binned said a-very-tall. I are planning to keep this up now. Rubber ring collecting is very actual quite MUCH betterer than sit.

4 December 2014

I are not completely sure who my ears do belong to because I do not be having any control over them at all. At first, Mum wondered if I was growing into my ears but now she does fink my ears are taking on a life of their own.

I can do a great impression of Elvis with a quiff. Other times I do look like a rabbit. When my ears go all floppy I do look like a teddy bear and I can very actual quite turn both my ears inside out - at the same time or one on its own. My ears could win Britain's Got Talent all on their own.

I are very quite the master of disguise. I think that with my ears I have actual missed my calling. I should have binned a spy-dog. I could have the code name 00-Woo. Or be Worzel Bond. I do never look like the same dog twice.

The baddies could be asking for my description and they would all be very confuddled.

Perhaps my ears do be remote controlled by someone actual very else? If it is you, could you please be leaving them in one position for a bit because it is quite very fiddly wandering about with parts of your boddedy doing strange fings all the time. Thanking you kindly. Worzel Wooface... Bond.

6 December 2014

Wot's worse than eating a book? Eating the very actual one Mum is currently reading. Honestly, she is making such a big, blinking fuss HAND I lefted her most of the bit she hasn't read yet. Happarently, Charlotte at the library isn't going to feel the same actual way.

7 December 2014

There is lots of talk happening at the moment about Christmas. The previously ginger one is in-very-charge of Christmas this year because Mum is too busy trying to organise a Panty Mine and Dad says Christmas starts on Christmas Eve which is ok 'if you're a man who just expects everything to happen by magic.'

Dad reckons he would be quite happy if it didn't happen at all, seeing as Leeds lost again yesterday and it's not high on his list of priorities. At this point everyone scuttled off and left Dad to his sulk and got on with horganising it around him.

The talk at the moment is about Christmas Trees and whether to have a real tree or a fake one. I find this quite very confuddling. I do not know how you can have a fake tree. It is either a tree or not a tree. Mum has seen some hinteresting trees made of other fings like step ladders which she fort were very stylish but this did cause the previously ginger one to flap and breathe funny because That. Is. Not. A. Tree. So, a fake tree IS a tree but somefing pretending to be a tree is NOT a tree. Dad wants a real tree but he is not In Charge and do not be wanting to think about Christmas until he has got over the Leeds fing so he is mostly being hignored.

I do not be finking fakery should be the number one topic when actual talking about Christmas trees. I would like to talk about why a perfickly reasonable fing like a tree, wot does belong outside, is coming hinside. Trees is for, well, erm... peeing up. And trees are like hooman Facebook. Us dogs do be getting all our gossip off trees and I do wonder how a hindoor tree wot gets no visitors can be communercating with the rest of the world. A hindoor tree is like a confuser without wifi. Happarently I do not be being allowed to pee up the hindoor tree; I do not fink this will be a problem because if no-one else has pee'd up it there won't be any very actual real point.

Mum would like a small 'real' tree or a step ladder tree, one wot can sit up high out of the way. The previously ginger one wants a 'fake' one the size of a caravan because this is proper and She. Is. In. Charge. Dad temporarily gived up on not getting hinvolved at this point and said the previously ginger one could get wotever she liked if it meant he could carry on watching the Leeds press conference and if it meant Mum wasn't going to do something all weird and creative with his step ladder.

Now, I do not be wanting to get my bestest cat Gandhi into trouble or nuffink but everyboddedy seems to be avoiding this helefant in the room. You may be thinking that a small tabby kitten wot is cute and luffly cannot be compared to an helefant but if you do take one fuge Christmas tree, cover it in a gazillion pretty baubly fings and wafty tinsel, then add one tabby kitten to the mix, you is going to have a very actual disaster the size of 3 helefants, not just one.

I do not be knowing how this is going to end. The Christmas tree is arriving on Tuesday and I will let you know wot it do look like. And how long it do be staying hupright. I fink I will be staying out of the sitting room where it is being put unless Gandhi do look like he is thinking of climbing it, in which case it will be my very actual duty to stop him. Cos that would be the right fing to do, wouldn't it?

9 December 2014

Today, Dad came for a walk with us. Dad can't come for a walk very actual often because he has to do that work fing. It is most hinconvenient, you know.

So, we wented for a walk and it was quite very exerlent and then I did sawed a deer. Usually Dad spots deers before me and I is not much of a chaser anyway but today, with the wind being all blowy up my actual bum and me being all hexcited cos Dad was with us, I did show off and try to chase the deer.

The deer was in no danger because it was on the other side of a fence wot I could not get through. But whilst I was gettering over-hexcited I did hurt myself. I did limping. And lying down. AND shaking. I was very chilly as well because I had been in my puddle play area earlier so I was cold and sore and Mum was very quite actual hupset.

Mum told Dad he was going to have to carry me. Dad did look at me and I did look at him with my bestest I'm-cold-and-sad-and-miserababble-and-my-leg-does-hurt-a-lot-and-a-very-quite-actual-lot face. I are not as good at faces as Merlin. Merlin woulda binned picked up on 'I'm-cold...' but then Merlin weighs about a half of a quarter of wot I do.

I hobviously need some more actual lessons from Merlin on 'I'm sad...' faces because Dad did then try to persuade Mum that I was very going to be fine and dandy if we did just do waiting about in the cold for a minute. I do not know who he fort he was kidding but I do know he was very actual flinching at the fort of carrying me one whole mile back to our house

When Mum wants to be, she can be actual quite scary so Dad did decide that this was not the moment to try to reason with Mum and did pick me up. Mum wrapped her coat around me after a while because the wind was in my face and I was shakering.

Dad did nearly do himself his own hinjury carrying me. I do weigh 26kg which is 4 stone in old money. Dad says that I is a blinking heavy cold wet dog to have to carry into the wind but we maded it home to the warm where I was quite actual glad to be.

You can tell I was proper hurted because I did not do Complaints to the Management when Mum feeled me all over to find out wot was wrong. And do you know wot is wrong? No? Neither does Mum because apart from me walking a bit stiff and flat-footed she cannot find one single fing wrong with me. But I is not quite myself. I are definitely sore, we just can't work out where.

10 December 2014

So the good news is that I has been for a run and my leg is all betterer. Mum does think it was cramp. The bad news is that in all the hexcitement of me showing Mum that I is all not sore now, I did forget to look where I was going and Mum was too busy looking at me for signs of limps or wobbling, that she forgotted to remember where I actual was compared to where she was. So I did run into Mum and now she has the bruise the size of Wales on her knee.

12 December 2014

Me and the Christmas tree are on good terms so far. I has mostly left it alone and it has not frightened me a-very-tall. This is mainly because it is staying in hexactly the same spot all the time and not making any sudden moves.

I did know this tree hindoors fing was going to cause trouble though. One of the cats has decided that seeing as there is a tree in the sitting room, it's hobviously part of the garden and did do a poo behind it. Mum is not best pleased but she is relieved she found out before I did.

13 December 2014

If you do bite the head off an angel do you go on Father Christmas's naughty list?

Even if it was left on the floor by Gandhi? Even if it was VERY quite actual proper ugly? Or does that make it worse because Father Christmas's spies will feel sorry for the weird, red, ugly angel with a square cushion tummy and an ex-wooden head wot I has now very actual chewed to actual bits?

14 December 2014

We have a British roundabout situation here. You know that very actual fing when 3 cars do approach a roundabout at hexactly the same time and there's this confuddledness cos no-one knows who should go first and who is going to be blamed if everyone goes at once and there is a big accident...

Well.... Early this morning, a man wot Mum does know, who is a bit anxious about dogs, camed to drop some stuff off. Mum knows that when I meet people who is scared of me, I get scared of them and it all turns into a barking, twitchy worry fest, so she did quickly hencourage me upstairs, into the previously ginger one's bedroom and shutted the door. I was not very actual himpressed with this course of action and neither was the previously ginger one who was still very quite still asleep. She was not amused when I did jump on her and told me to 'Geroff' and then shouted 'what the hell are you doing shut in here hanyway... Muuuum!' But that was not the worst of it.

I do not know if I was cross at being shutted in the previously ginger one's room, or whether I did be suddenly wanting to go outside OR if I was hupset cos the previously ginger one told me to 'Geroff her bed' but when the visitor did go, the previously ginger one letted out this most ignormous arghhy-squealing noise. Cos when I stooded up there was a fuge wet patch on the duvet. Under me. All warm and smelling of dog.

So now everyone is saying fings like 'Why the heckington stanley did you do that?' 'Why did Wooface do a wee on the bed?' 'Why did Mum shut poor me in the bedroom?' 'Why didn't the previously ginger one notice before it did happen?'

Like I was very saying, this is one of those British roundabout situations.

Trouble is, Mum is very quite British and so she is the actual sort of person to wait at a roundabout saying hafter-very-you. The previously ginger one might be British but she is a teenager wot does overrule everyfing, I is not British, I is a dog. So me and the previously ginger one are sulking on Mum's bed and she's doing her bestest British stiff-upper-lip himpression whilst she clears up the mess.

17 December 2014

I are not speaking to Mum. Today she hadded one of her most stoopidest ideas hever, ever.

I do hoccasionally have a habit of going for a mooch on our walks. By mooch, I do mean belt off at 30mph after a crow or somefing. We do walk in safe places but Mum does sometimes get bored of yelling 'Woor-zel' and then discovering I are only 20 ft away and having a cunning roll in some fox poo.

So, she got this BELL and Put. It. On. My. Collar. So she could hear where I was. I did have a very actual hissy fit. I did do trying to run away from the noisy fing and trying to get out of my collar and everyfing.

Mum did quickly take it off. I was not a happy Worzel a-very-tall.

But I has solved the problem. Mum can wear the bell and tinkle away nicely and she can carry on yelling and tinkling and when I hear this I will do coming back very-nicely-thank-you-kindly-where's-my-cheese.

But I will not be doing wearing a bell. I is not a cow, this is not Switzerland and Mum is not called Heidi.

18 December 2014

Somebodded has actual very played a trick on me and when I do find out who it quite is, they is going to be feeding me sausages for a actual whole month.

When we did go for our walk today, everyfing was fantastic. I did do showing off walking and waiting and remembering not to jump about like a hysterical stallion on the way to the start of the Grand National. I was a very, very exerlent boykin. I even managed to do sitting and waiting before 'off you go' even though Merlin was trying to jump up and lick my eyeballs.

It has binned a luffly day here, the sun has binned all shiny and bright and just perfick for major runnings about, wot me and Merlin did do. A couple of times I did fink of bogging off but I did exerlent Come-waggy-tails-kisses-for everyboddedy, even though there was no cheese.

But, very actual blinking BUT... someboddedy did somefing to my play puddle. I was screeching along at the speed of Frank when Mum do open the fridge, then I leaped into the very air, hexpecting a super muddy splash and I did hit somefing HARD and cold and very, very quite actual slippery. My legs did go in 7 different directions, I did bash my head and slided along on my back. I did hurted my leg and as for my very actual diggernatty, I don't fink I do be having any of that left.

Merlin did get to me first. He looked at me as if I was a stoopid crazy boykin. Mum came rushing up to me saying all kinds of soppy Wooface noises but I did just look at her like she had turned everyfing hupside down. I did do having a major limping sulk-fest.

Mum did not do laughing, she says. She did check me out and apart from being muddy, she says I are ok. But I is NOT OK. IT IS NOT FAIR. I want my puddle back. Except I do not be liking puddles now and I do be finking they are all dangerous and scary and I feel like I has been betrayed by my bestest toy hever.

22 December 2014

It's three days before Christmas and everyfing, haccording to the previously ginger one, has to be warm and fuzzy and Christmassy whether Dad likes it or not. Everyboddedy has to be luffly to each other and stop nicking all the candy canes off the Christmas tree. Singing carols is hoptional but listening to hawful songs on the radio is actual very not. We is all trying to do wot the previously ginger one says because she is In Charge of Christmas and although she's a lot betterer since Southampton and the Opital, she's not completely actual fixed so it's himportant everyfing goes well.

But everyfing is not all warm and fuzzy and going well in one area and there's a very lot of fibbing happening. The previously ginger one is all in a panic about Gandhi and she do fink he is poorly-sick because he did not eat his dinner tonight. Noboddedy wants to tell the previously ginger one why or how they do know he isn't sick because she finks he is her perfick, ickle baby-wabey and a cute, cuddly, Christmas kitty-witty.

He isn't. He's a murderous baby bunny muncher. Yesterday, Mum had to deal with a fuge not-sharing-nicely-gimme-a-bit hargument between several of the cats because he came home with a baby bunny wot he had caughted and didn't feel like sharing. He hidded under the water butt in the garden and hissed and hargued with Gipsy and Frank about it being his and no-he-didn't need-any-help-eatering-it.

Dad's finally managed to persuade the previously ginger one that it's probabbly a 24 hour bug and he has promised her that if Gandhi is not better by tomorrow, then of course Mum will take him to the vet.

The fuge ginger boyman has locked the cat-flap so he can't get out to catch another one and refuse to eat again tomorrow. Everyboddedy has hagreed that the previously ginger one has worked too very actual hard to make everyfing all perfick for Christmas; she can face the reality that Gandhi is a baby bunny basher when Boxing Day is over.

24 December 2014

Mum says that she doesn't need to wait for Gandhi to go chasing lady cats now. If he's big enough to catch a baby rabbit, he's big enough to have his gentleman bits removed.

I has had a measure and a check and I can actual confirm that since Gandhi has binned getting his takeaway bunnies, he has gotted fat and much, much longerer. As I couldn't catch a rabbit if I did get written permission from the Queen, I do fink Gandhi is probabbly a betterer Sighthound than I will hever be in that department. He'll never be able to take up as much room on the bed as me but last night he did decide to do lying on top of Dad with his bum under his chin which Dad did find very actual most hinconvenient and hunpleasant. I fink I can fishally declare him an Onorable Lurcher.

27 December 2014

I was very actual going to write about Christmas Day today but very actual events has been overtaking me. I will do writing about Christmas once the current dramas are actual over.

Hunlike Gandhi, who was pretend-sick-cos-he-did-eat-a-bunny, Gipsy has been very actual proper poorly-sick. She has been doing coughing and purring and all sorts. When Gipsy-the-Cat is happy she does bog off and catch mice and be an actual grumpy, bossy, scratch monster. She honly purrs when there is somefing very actual quite wrong.

Gipsy is so actual unwell, that she did let me get on the bed with her. I did not very quite believe her at first and stooded and whined a lot. Then I did put one foot on the bed and she did not attack me like a ninja-freaking-furball of hell so I did lie down next to her. And she did not be telling me off or nuffink. I has been being very gentle and kind to her and I do actual fink she and I has comed to a hunderstanding.

Mum says she do have a chest hinfection and Boris-the-Vet from Wangford has given her medicine and a hinjection. Gipsy-the-Cat did give Boris-the-Vet a fuge puddle on wee of his floor but then he did deserve it cos he stucked somefing up her bum wot she did not like. At all.

I fink when Gipsy is betterer, she and I might actual be friends cos I has been so luffly to her. Dad says I are being gullerble and he will know Gipsy is betterer again when Worzel gets bonked on the nose and chased down the actual stairs.

<u>29 December 2014</u>

Gipsy the cat is nearly betterer. She is shouting at everyone again and very actual being bossy. I do be hoping she does remember I was kind to her when she was poorly sick but Dad does say she has a very quite short memory for that actual kind of fing. I is taking his hadvices and staying out of bopping range. I do not need boppering at the actual moment because I did manage to bop my very actual self in the woods a couple of days ago and I do has a bit of a scrape and bruise. It does not hurt and I is barely noticing it now, fanking you kindly.

<u>30 December 2014</u>

Now that Gipsy is quite very bopperingly better, and now that our Christmas is almost quite nearly over, I fort I would tell you all about it. I cannot be saying if my Christmas was exerlent or not because it is the only one I can remember.

I do not know how Father Christmas did get into the house because I did not hear him. There was big sacks on the ends of the beds for Dad, the fuge ginger boyman and the previously ginger but there was not one for Mum. Dad did say this was because Mum was naughty but Mum does say that it was because Dad does his shopping on Christmas Eve like a maniac, panic machine and he isn't good on minor details. Later on in the day though there was a very expensive pair of new boots for Mum from Dad. I has had a serious talking to about not finking they is somefing I can actual chew. They costed Dad over a fundred pounds and if I eat them, he says he will do crying.

We did work out who was most confuddled about the hindoor tree fing. It was Mouse wot did do a poo behind the tree. We do know this because Dad caughted her trying to do it again. He did chase her out of the room and call her all sorts of rude names, none of which was Mouse and lots of them did begin with B.

Gandhi managed to stay out of the Christmas tree until Boxing Dad when Dad did decide that he wanted more light in the room and tooked the lamp shade off the light in the middle of the ceiling. He decided it would be funny to put it on the top of the Christmas tree. Dad does not be making the bestest decisions when he has had a drink of cider; the lampshade did make the tree too top heavy and all the decorations wobbled and shimmered wot was too much for Gandhi to resist. Up went Gandhi, down went the tree and I did have a small hissy fit because it was all quite loud and scary. There was tinsel and baubles and balls everywhere.

Talking of balls, Gandhi don't be having any no more. He wented to see Uncle Boris yesterday, had a nice sleep and woked up lighter around the trouser department. Mum was told to keep him in for 3 days. He hescaped after 3 minutes. Mum did lose some brownie points for that.

I did get a Christmas present wot is fantastic. It is a squeaky fish and I still hasn't deaded it. This has surprised everyboddedy here because usually I do dead toys in about 3 minutes. Nemo, I are finding, is much more blinking tough than he looks.

I has enjoyed Christmas very actual much because everyboddedy has been at home and there has been plenty of time and attention for Worzel Wooface. The previously ginger one did a fabumazing job of being In Charge and she maded sure there was lots of compnee and not much rushering about, plenty of actual very nice treats and lots of snoozering in front of the fire.

31 December 2014

Tonight I has been to a Noo Near Party wot hoomans do have at the end of the year. At a Noo Near Party hoomans do drink everyfing they has got lefted from Christmas so that they can start again in the Noo Near.

It wasn't one of them 'You can bring your dog if you has to,' parties and it wasn't a doggy party either. It was a hooman party and then there was this phone call asking if me, Worzel Wooface, would very actual hattend.

Mum did say 'Yes please!' for me, although she didn't do telling me I had get in a minibus to go, which did nearly put the kibosh on the whole night. How-very-ever, there was a bit of picking up and plonkering of me in the minibus and that was quite that.

When we did get to the party there was 11 hoomans and 4 dogs as well as me. All the other dogs were black Labrador type dogs wot Dad did fink all looked the same but that was because he had too much Cider and not enuff dog sense.

Herbie was a senior Sir Doggy, and he was quite clear that me, as a junior toe-rag was going to be doing as I was very actual quite told. Some of the hoomans did be very worrying about this but I was an exerlent boykin and did remember my pleases and my thank yous and my flipping-'eck-you-may-be-blind-but-you-is-scary-I-will-be-doing-as-you-do-say-Sir-thanking-you-kindly. Simba, Lola and Sam from Dad's work were also at the party. Sam mostly liked me to mooch about with him but Lola and Simba wanted to very actual play. We did make up a game where I did run fast and they did try to corner me, then I did play bow and they did bow and then we did do it again... and again... and again. It was very actual quite fabumazing and sweaty and panting-making.

Mum is very quite protective of me, I dunno if you has noticed and so I has not binned allowed to 'sociate with dogs wot are unpredictababble in case they do be bashing my confidence but tonight I did show off how much of a super luffly boykin I are at reading other doggy's hinstructions, even when those hinstructions are you-is-a-whipper-snapper-Wooface-even-if-you-is-the-very-actual-size-of-a-table.

After we had done running about in the garden, I did quietly confident with lots of new peoples, and mainly coping with hunexpected loud bangs and very actual proper not reacting to people moving fast or worrying about wot was going on around me. I mostly stucked near Mum and Dad and when I couldn't see them for a little bit, I wented and laid down on the sofa and did chillering and very not worrying at all.

Everyboddedy had nice fings to say about Worzel Wooface, even the ones who were drinking orange juice. People keeped saying I was amazing and gentle and special but mainly wasn't it fantastic how far I had actual come in a year.

Mum was hunbelievababbly proud of me and I are hoping that if fings continue like this maybe, just maybe, I might get treated like a nearly normal actual dog in 2015.

Dad says there is no chance of me HEVER being treated like a nearly normal dog. He says I just has to haccept the fact that I are Worzel Wooface and I are quite simply a quite very actual superstar.

ABOUT THE AUTHOR

Worzel Wooface is a Hounds First Sighthound Rescue dog. He likes walking, spending time with his family and chasing crows when given the opportunity. His current hobby is chewing wellies on unmade beds. He lives in Suffolk.

Catherine Pickles is a full-time family carer, writer and blogger. Her blog about Worzel reached the final of the UK Blog Awards in 2015.
She likes sailing, walking, gardening and amateur dramatics. She likes doing most of these things with Worzel (apart from gardening but she doesn't have much choice about it and the amateur dramatics which he would hate). She lives in Suffolk with her husband, 2 nearly grown up children and 5 cats.

USEFUL LINKS

worzelwooface.co.uk
facebook.com/WorzeltheLurcher
@Worzel_Wooface

houndsfirst.co.uk
harbourmarine.co.uk
stovenhallvets.co.uk
wangfordvetclinic.com
facebook.com/ReydonAndSouthwoldPantomimeGroup
life-changingchallenges.co.uk

12089775R00122

Printed in Great Britain
by Amazon.co.uk, Ltd.,
Marston Gate.